IMPERFECT ENVIRONMENTALISM

Revolutionizing Every Transaction Into Climate Action

Nidhi Mehra
Koushik Sur

BlueRose ONE
Stories Matter
New Delhi • London

BLUEROSE PUBLISHERS
India | U.K.

For permissions requests or inquiries regarding this publication,
please contact:

BLUEROSE PUBLISHERS
www.BlueRoseONE.com
info@bluerosepublishers.com
+91 8882 898 898
+4407342408967

ISBN: 978-93-7310-149-1

Cover design: Aafiya Saifi
Typesetting: Manisha Rawat

First Edition: December 2025

Disclaimer

The concepts, frameworks, scoring systems, methodologies, narrative structures, intellectual property, and technological philosophies described throughout this book—including the Green People Score, Green Business Score, Environmental Quotient, Climate Intelligence Layer, and the Imperfect Environmentalism model—are original innovations created and developed by the founders of ***Myplan8®****.*

While this book presents these ideas in a narrative and educational form for global understanding, the underlying intellectual property, associated technologies, scoring logic, algorithms, interpretive methods, and process architectures remain the exclusive proprietary creations of the Myplan8® founding team.

No part of these systems may be replicated, reproduced, adapted, or commercialized in any form without explicit written permission from the founders.

The purpose of this book is to share the philosophy behind the innovation, inspire systemic change, and empower individuals, businesses, and institutions to take meaningful steps toward environmental responsibility. The ownership of all ideation, formulation, and theoretical constructs described herein rests solely with the founders of Myplan8®.

Thank You Note

This book speaks to the dreamers and disruptors alike-the wonderfully curious souls who see patterns others miss and dare to question what no one else thinks to question. It also honours parents like ours, who never quenched that curiosity but nourished it, helping us grow into adults who question norms rather than simply inherit them. And it celebrates spouses like ours, who stay steady when we step away from safe, predictable careers into uncertain ideas, providing the grounding that makes bold risks possible. This is for the builders and thinkers of our generation-the millennials and Gen Z creators whose innovations have shaped our world. Their work sometimes fuelled excess, yet it always demonstrated the power of imagination. Imperfect Environmentalism redirects that imagination toward something larger and more enduring-a belief that imperfect people, when guided by the right hands and driven by the right questions, can change the world one choice at a time.

🌍 Prelude — Two Imperfect Minds, One Realisation

They didn't set out to build a climate movement.

They didn't even begin start by talking about the planet.

They started as two professionals — one from marketing, one from finance and product development — who kept stumbling upon a truth hiding in plain sight.

Let's call them Ms. Imperfect and Mr. Imperfect.

Ms. Imperfect spent more than twenty years mastering the art of influence — campaigns that could shift consumption overnight, ideas that could turn browsing into buying, and buying into habit. But beneath the achievements was a quiet discomfort. She deeply believed in sustainability, yet she was part of the machinery that made people want more, buy more, and think less.

Before COVID ever arrived, she made a decision rooted in clarity:

If you want to understand behaviour, you must understand money.

So, she stepped deliberately into the Indian fintech space — not as a trend-follower, but as someone who wanted to learn how financial systems shape people just as deeply as advertising does.

On the other side stood Mr. Imperfect, a certified financial planner who had built fintech products from scratch — not decks, not ideas, but real systems. He was a young founder, a product architect, someone who understood both the human and the coded layers of finance.

If Ms. Imperfect could read behaviour, he could quantify it.

If she saw patterns in people, he saw patterns in money.

Their worlds collided during the Indian fintech boom, and conversations that began as product discussions soon expanded into long, curious debates about spending, saving, digital habits, and the invisible forces guiding modern life.

And then came the moment that shifted everything.

🍎 The Apple Realisation — Their "Newton Moment"

Like Newton's apple falling on his head and revealing gravity, their moment of clarity also began with an Apple — just not the fruit.

A colleague had walked in proudly showing off the latest iPhone.

Ms. Imperfect laughed and said,

"Congratulations on your new depreciating jewellery. iPhones lose value the moment the box opens."

Mr. Imperfect didn't contradict her — he refined it.

He explained the true depreciation curve, the resale behaviour, the rise of apple finance for consumer affordability driving their market share and then added something she hadn't fully considered:

"When you compare devices by environmental footprint, Apple phones are greener than most Android devices. Not because of marketing — but because Apple does the actual work. Material recovery. Carbon-neutral manufacturing. Energy-efficient processes. Real ESG discipline."

Apple wasn't sustainable because it sold a phone.

Or Apple wasn't sustainable because they built a finance system around it.

It was sustainable because compliance was need by global brand and **it built a financial system AND a sustainability system around the device**, making it environmentally responsible even as the gadget itself depreciated in a user's hand.

A depreciating asset for the pocket —

an environmentally neutralised asset for the planet.

The contradiction made perfect sense.

Financial value and environmental value rarely move together —

but behavioural awareness and climate impact always do.

And if a company could build responsibility into a device ecosystem,

why couldn't individuals learn the impact of their own daily choices?

That question didn't leave the room.

It followed them.

From Insight to Intention

Their conversations deepened.

They pored over global data, ESG frameworks, climate research, and consumer psychology.

They built surveys — not generic ones, but personal ones — and while Ms. Imperfect reached out to her **IIM alumni** Mr. Imperfect tapped into the brains of his **ISB alumnus**.

One question was intentionally simple:

"If tomorrow you had to live fully green — would you turn vegan?"

Both of them laughed because they knew their own answers: *No. Definitely, May be*

They enjoyed their food, their lifestyle, and knew they weren't going to transform overnight.

And that was the insight they needed.

People don't avoid responsibility —

it's just difficult to change your own choices, even when you care.

Sustainability wasn't lacking because people were unwilling.

It was lacking because the choices were emotionally, culturally, and practically complex.

And complexity always loses to convenience.

So, they asked a better question:

What if sustainability didn't require a lifestyle overhaul?

What if it simply required awareness?

💡 The Turning Point

They analysed global behaviour shifts.

They studied how fintech had made investing accessible.

They noticed how the simplest dashboard could change a lifetime habit.

They saw that people behave differently the moment numbers become visible.

And that led to the foundational realisation:

People don't change because they are told to.

People change because they can *see* the impact.

Visibility, not moral pressure, was missing.

So, they quit their jobs.

Not impulsively — intentionally.

They wanted to build something that connected modern life with climate responsibility, not through guilt or sacrifice, but through design, behaviour, intelligence, and clarity.

Over the next two years, they explained this thinking inside one of India's largest public sector banks. Meeting after meeting, deck after deck, they heard the same confusion:

"We understand sustainability.

We understand banking.

But how do the two actually meet?"

And that's when they realised the world didn't just need a product.

It needed a **philosophy**.

A way to see the climate impact in the everyday.

A story that made the invisible visible.

A way to understand that the smallest decision —

a swipe, a tap, a purchase —

moves the world in one direction or another.

🌎 Why This Book Exists

Not to preach.

Not to demand perfection.

Not to advocate dramatic lifestyle changes.

But to reveal a simple truth:

Every transaction is already a climate action —

you just haven't been shown how.

This book exists to make that connection clear.

To show how imperfect people — not perfect systems — shape the future.

To make climate awareness as intuitive as checking your bank balance.

To help readers understand the hidden impact behind their daily behaviour.

It is the story of Ms. Imperfect and Mr. Imperfect —

two minds who realised that you don't need to be perfect to make a difference.

You just need to be aware.

Welcome to their story.

Welcome to your story.

Welcome to **Imperfect Environmentalism**.

Contents

Part I

The World We Inherited

Chapter 1:

A Perfect World Full Of Imperfect People

If you close your eyes and imagine the beginning of our modern world, you'll hear a sound long before you see anything: the deep, rolling whistle of a steam engine. That whistle didn't just announce a machine passing through; it marked humanity stepping onto an entirely new track—one that moved faster than anything nature had ever needed to recover from.

Sometimes, that moment feels like an iceberg in my mind—majestic and shimmering above the surface, hiding an immense, invisible weight beneath. The Industrial Revolution gave us the glittering part we loved to look at: comfort, speed, innovation, power. But beneath all that brilliance, a cost was quietly accumulating, layer by unseen layer.

And as with every iceberg, the danger wasn't in what we could see.

It was in what we chose not to.

Those coal furnaces, steam engines, and early factories transformed us into creators of abundance. Humanity travelled farther, produced more, lived longer, and achieved what earlier generations could never imagine. But alongside progress, something subtle happened too—something no one could articulate at the time.

We normalized excess.

Machines began moving faster than forests could regrow, faster than rivers could cleanse themselves, faster than the earth could buffer our ambition. A tiny imbalance crept into our trajectory. Just a degree off-course. Barely noticeable. Harmless-looking. But stay one degree off long enough, and you land somewhere you never intended to be.

Our ancestors weren't irresponsible.

They were enchanted.

Enthralled by what felt like magic.

A machine doing the work of fifty people.

A train outrunning a galloping horse.

A bulb replacing fire.

Progress seemed synonymous with promise. Growth looked like hope itself.

But while gears turned above the surface, something else was turning below: a slow accumulation of emissions, extraction, and invisible consequences that would take centuries to fully reveal themselves.

Today, when we see fractured glaciers, sweltering cities, displaced seasons, and charts climbing in the wrong direction, it feels as if the earth has finally spoken in a voice too loud to ignore. The signs were always there—we were simply too mesmerized by the gleam of the surface to notice the mass forming unnoticed beneath.

This chapter isn't here to scold our past.

It's here to illuminate a simple truth:

The world we inherited wasn't built by villains.

It was built by imperfect humans, just like us.

People who acted with limited information.

People who made choices shaped by the systems available to them.

People who genuinely believed they were building a better world.

And that changes everything.

Because once you understand this, you begin to see sustainability differently—not as a moral test reserved for flawless people who get everything right but as a journey of awareness for all the imperfect people who simply want to do better.

Perfection is exhausting.

And rare.

And unnecessary.

Most people aren't unwilling.

They're overwhelmed.

They want to make good choices, but they live inside systems optimized for convenience, speed, and consumption. They juggle work, family, finances, emotions, and expectations. And in that swirl of demands, sustainability can feel like yet another impossible responsibility.

Expecting perfection from imperfect humans, living inside imperfect structures, isn't just unrealistic—

it's unproductive.

This is something Ms. Imperfect and Mr. Imperfect understood long before they built anything together. In one of their earliest conversations, Ms. Imperfect had sighed and said, "If the planet needed perfect people to save it, we would have lost this battle a century ago."

Mr. Imperfect laughed softly and replied, "Exactly. The world doesn't need perfect behaviour. It needs consistent behaviour—even if it's flawed."

That sentence lingered.

Because it was true.

Millions of imperfect people doing a little will always create more change than a handful of perfect people doing a lot.

Climate progress isn't linear.

It's cyclical—a loop of awareness → intention → distraction → correction → improvement.

A loop every human being lives.

And that loop is not evidence of human weakness.

It is evidence of human reality.

Two Mindsets: The Solver and the Finder

Over time, they also noticed something else: people oscillate between two mindsets.

The Solver

The mindset that says, "Maybe I can't fix everything, but what can I do today?"

This is the instinct our grandparents embodied—repairing instead of replacing, stretching resources, valuing durability, and reducing waste out of wisdom, not trendiness.

The Finder

The mindset that says, "It's too complicated. Someone else will handle it."

Not out of carelessness, but because life already feels full and fragile and fast.

Most of us aren't one or the other—we are both, shifting like tides depending on the day, the mood, the capacity, the chaos around us.

Imperfect Environmentalism isn't about eliminating the Finder.

It's about gently nudging the Finder toward the Solver just a little more often—through visibility, convenience, intelligence, and design.

A New Way of Seeing Ourselves

And so, the philosophy begins:

Environmental action isn't a test of purity.

It is a practice of awareness.

You don't need a zero-waste lifestyle.

You don't need perfect habits.

You don't need to eliminate every footprint you leave behind.

You only need one foundational skill:

the ability to see the invisible cost behind your choices.

Once you see it, you begin to adjust.

Not perfectly.

Not always.

But steadily enough to matter.

And that is the entire foundation of this book.

We inherited a world built on imperfect choices.

Now it's our turn to build a future on better ones.

Not flawlessly.

Not instantly.

But consciously.

Because the world does not need perfect environmentalists.

It needs billions of imperfect people—aware, willing, and ready to begin.

Chapter 2:

Understanding Your Carbon Footprint

If the previous chapter helped us understand the world we inherited, this one helps us understand the world we quietly create every day without realising it. Not the world outside, but the invisible world trailing behind us like a shadow — the world of carbon emissions.

We don't hear it.

We don't feel it.

But it follows us all the same.

And for most people, awareness doesn't begin with a documentary or a data chart. It begins with something small and ordinary — like a cup of coffee.

The Coffee That Became a Lesson

A few months ago, Ms. Imperfect met a friend at a café for a quick catch-up. Nothing unusual — just two women decompressing from their week.

Her friend ordered a tall caramel latte, the kind that feels like a tiny festival in a cup.

"It's my comfort drink," she said, smiling.

"Please don't tell me the calories. I already know I shouldn't be having it."

Ms. Imperfect laughed.

"I'm not talking about calories."

"Oh?" her friend teased. "Then what warning label does this cup come with?"

"A different C," Ms. Imperfect said.

"Not calories. Carbon emissions."

Her friend blinked at the cup.

"Are you trying to make me feel guilty?"

"No," Ms. Imperfect replied gently.

"I'm trying to help you see the story behind it. Once you know that story, your choices change — not perfectly, but naturally."

That softened her friend.

"Alright… tell me. What's the story?"

So, she did. Without drama, without jargon — simply and honestly.

She described how those coffee beans were grown, irrigated, harvested, processed, dried, shipped across continents, roasted, packed, delivered, ground, brewed… and finally poured into a paper cup lined with plastic resin and topped with a lid that would likely outlive both of them.

Her friend exhaled.

"So, this one latte carries all that with it?"

"It's not about the latte," Ms. Imperfect said.

"It's about noticing the invisible part of everything in your day."

That conversation stayed with her friend — not because it was shocking, but because it made sense.

Clarity often does.

The Invisible That Shapes Our Days

Carbon emissions don't shout.

They don't leave footprints you can touch.

They behave like the underside of an iceberg — massive, shaping everything, yet fully hidden from view.

We grew up learning to check prices.

We were never taught to check impact.

If emissions appeared in red ink the way calories appear on food labels, we would live very differently. But carbon was never designed to be visible, and so we move through life unaware of the invisible weight of our choices.

Not because anyone is deceiving us —

but because modern systems were created long before visibility mattered.

Carbon Emissions in Human Language

When people hear the word "emissions," they imagine smokestacks or scientific diagrams. But in everyday life, emissions are simply the after-effects of energy.

Electricity has an after-effect.

Transport has an after-effect.

Food, clothing, devices, entertainment — all of them do.

Some are light.

Some are heavy.

Some depend entirely on the source.

You don't see these emissions, but your lifestyle carries them — consistently, quietly, and without your permission.

It's not a burden.

It's a pattern.

If the Planet Took Notes for 24 Hours

Imagine the planet keeping a soft notebook of your day, not to judge you, but to observe.

Your morning shower?

Heated water powered by energy sources you didn't choose.

Your phone?

Mining → manufacturing → global shipping → daily charging.

Your short video break?

Data centres → servers → cooling systems → electricity.

Your dinner?

Cold storage → transport → packaging → preparation.

Every item has a history.

Every action has a ripple.

Not because you designed the system,

but because you stepped into it.

You Didn't Create the System — You Inherited It

Your carbon footprint is not a moral rating.

It isn't proof of whether you're a "good" or "bad" person.

It is simply a reflection of the world you were born into — a world shaped by industrial choices you didn't make.

You didn't decide how your electricity is generated.

You didn't select your city's transport grid.

You didn't design global supply chains.

Your footprint mirrors history, not personal failure.

And this distinction matters, because:

Awareness is not accusation.

Awareness is agency.

Why Awareness Changes Everything

When Ms. Imperfect's friend finally understood the "invisible story" of her latte, she didn't feel ashamed.

She felt informed.

And informed people behave differently.

Not radically.

Not perfectly.

But consciously.

That's the essence of imperfect environmentalism:

small shifts driven by clear sight.

Carbon emissions aren't shown to punish you.

They're shown so you can finally see the threads connecting your life to the planet's.

You can't redirect what you can't see.

But once you can see it, direction becomes instinctive.

Imperfect Environmentalism Begins Here

A carbon footprint isn't a weight on your shoulders.

It's a map — a guide — an x-ray of the world behind your choices.

It helps you notice what you never saw.

It helps you adjust what you reasonably can.

It helps you take small, imperfect steps that accumulate over time.

And that is where imperfect environmentalism truly begins — not in giving up your coffee, not in living a zero-waste life, not in rearranging your entire existence.

It begins in a quiet moment of recognition.

A moment when the invisible becomes visible.

A moment when you make a slightly different choice because awareness has been unlocked.

Imperfect steps, taken consistently,

shape more change than perfect steps taken rarely.

Awareness is your first footprint.

Choice is your second.

Chapter 3:

Money: The Perfect Tool

Some ideas arrive slowly, over months or years. Others appear during casual conversations — the kind you don't intend to have but keep thinking about long after. For Ms. Imperfect and Mr. Imperfect, one such moment began not with finance, not with climate, but with movies.

Stories have a strange power. They hold truths that sit quietly inside us long before we can name them. And money — whether whispered, joked about, feared, or chased — has always been one of cinema's favourite truths. No matter the decade or the genre, money always found its way into the dialogue, into the meaning, into the lesson.

Ms. Imperfect began by recalling a memory from her childhood. She had watched *Hello, Dolly!* with her father, mesmerised more by the cadence of the scenes than the music. And in that musical whirl, she heard Barbra Streisand say:

"Money, pardon the expression, is like manure.

It's not worth a thing unless it's spread around, helping young things grow."

She didn't know why the line stayed with her.

But as an adult — someone who spent years shaping consumer behaviour — it suddenly felt prophetic.

Money was never meant to sit still.

It was meant to move, to enable, to nurture — to be a tool, not a trophy.

Years later, as a teenager, she found herself immersed in *Vanilla Sky*. Tom Cruise's dialogue struck her deeply — especially because her father had scribbled it in a notebook:

"What is the answer to ninety-nine out of a hundred questions? ... Money."

At fifteen, it sounded dramatic.

As an adult, it sounded uncomfortably accurate.

Not because money is everything.

But because money touches *everything*.

It shapes choices quietly — what we buy, how we live, what we chase, and what we avoid. Money is not loud. It is persistent.

Mr. Imperfect smiled at her recollection. His defining money moment came from a very different cinematic universe — *Fight Club*. Not the chaos and rebellion most people remember, but the truth hiding underneath:

"Advertising has us chasing cars and clothes,

working jobs, we dislike so we can buy things we don't need."

He had paused the movie the first time he heard it.

It was the moment he realised that money and influence had merged long before fintech existed.

And then came the line that lodged itself into his worldview:

"The things you own end up owning you."

Consumption didn't just shape identity — it gradually began *replacing* it.

They laughed through a list of iconic movie scenes — *Confessions of a Shopaholic, Sex and the City* — an era where closets became status symbols, credit cards became coping mechanisms, and buying became both entertainment and therapy.

But underneath the laughter lived a quiet recognition:

Money had always been the silent architect of human behaviour.

Movies weren't teaching anything new.

They were simply holding up mirrors.

And in that mirror, both of them saw the same truth from different angles:

Follow the trail of any human decision long enough,

and you eventually arrive at money.

Not because humans are greedy —

but because money is woven into modern life.

Everything we touch, choose, buy, use, save, waste, or desire passes through money first.

Money shapes comfort.

Comfort shapes behaviour.

Behaviour shapes emissions.

Emissions shape the future.

Which leads to something simple and significant:

Money quietly shapes the climate.

Not through activism or ideology,

but through the mathematics of everyday life.

Every swipe, every purchase, every subscription carries a story —

a story of energy, extraction, manufacturing, packaging, transport, and impact.

A story people never see because they're only taught to track the price tag —

not the planetary tag.

This chapter is not about guilt.

It's about recognition.

Because when Ms. Imperfect heard Dolly Levi talk about money spreading growth…

when she heard *Vanilla Sky* frame money as the answer to nearly everything…

and when Mr. Imperfect heard *Fight Club* warn how advertising manipulates desire…

They weren't just listening to movie lines anymore.

They were listening to the unfiltered truth of human behaviour.

Money influences people faster than climate warnings ever have.

And for the first time, their philosophies aligned.

Ms. Imperfect, who spent her life understanding *why* people buy,

and Mr. Imperfect, who spent his life building *how* people buy,

landed on the same realisation:

Money is the world's most powerful behavioural technology.

It shapes patterns.

It shapes demand.

It shapes dreams.

It shapes identity.

And without ever being designed for it,

it shapes carbon footprints.

Not because money is moral or immoral —

but because money is motivational.

People don't change because they're told to.

People change because something becomes easier, cheaper, rewarding, visible,

or aligned with who they believe they are.

Money sits at the centre of all these levers.

That's why we shifted from cash to UPI,

from paper forms to instant digital investments,

from monthly bills to real-time apps.

Not because humanity suddenly evolved —

but because money became frictionless.

So naturally, the question emerged:

If money can make investing effortless,

shopping instant,

transport seamless,

and consumption habitual…

What else could it make unproblematic?

Could money make climate action instinctive?

Could money help individuals understand their unseen emissions?

Could money bridge the gap between what we choose and what the planet feels?

These questions stayed with them — quietly, steadily — shaping everything that followed.

This chapter is not about financial systems or sustainability metrics.

It is about a truth hiding in plain sight:

Money guides behaviour.

Behaviour guides emissions.

Therefore, money can guide emissions.

Not perfectly.

Not forcefully.

But naturally — through awareness.

In a world where carbon footprints remain invisible,

money can make them visible.

And the moment something becomes visible,

it becomes actionable.

Money is not the enemy.

It is the instrument.

And now, perhaps for the first time in history,

we have the chance to use that instrument

to guide the world toward better choices.

Chapter 4:

Millennials & Gen Z: The Perfect Generation

Every generation carries memories.

Millennials and Gen Z carry *two* kinds — the gentle rhythm of a slower world and the dizzying pace of a digital one. This dual exposure doesn't confuse them; it equips them. They have lived through sustainability without calling it sustainability, and through convenience without questioning convenience.

And somewhere between these two worlds lies their quiet superpower.

A Childhood Rooted in Sustainability

Before words like *eco-friendly* or *zero-waste* became hashtags, this generation lived them naturally. Steel tiffins travelled to school every day, water came from refilled bottles, and grocery trips happened with cloth bags folded neatly inside handbags. Clothes lived multiple lives — first as outfits, then as hand-me-downs, then as dusters. Leftovers became next-day meals, and plastic, when it appeared at all, was treated like a last resort.

They didn't label any of this conscious living.

It was simply life — shaped by the rhythm of reduce, reuse, recycle, repurpose, long before the world turned these into acronyms and frameworks.

Then the World Shifted

As economies grew and technology accelerated, life changed. Malls appeared. Fast fashion exploded. Delivery apps arrived with the promise of comfort at your doorstep. Single-use became normal, and convenience quietly overtook mindfulness.

Sustainability didn't disappear — it simply got overshadowed. Not because people stopped caring but because habits were pulled toward the pace of modern life.

And yet, the early lessons did not vanish. They slipped into the subconscious — into what behavioural science calls **habit memory**, the quiet storage where childhood patterns wait to be triggered again.

Habit Memory: The Forgotten Strength

This resurfacing revealed itself during an ordinary moment. After a long workday, Ms. Imperfect automatically folded and saved the paper takeout bags; Mr. Imperfect rinsed and kept jars to reuse at home. They laughed because it felt familiar — like muscle memory from childhood.

"We're basically our parents," he joked.

"It never left us," she replied. "We just stopped noticing."

It was a reminder that this generation is not starting from zero. They are returning to something they already knew — something that once came naturally.

The Imperfect Loop We All Live In

Modern life pulls people into a predictable behavioural loop:

Intention → Distraction → Convenience → Correction → Return

This loop doesn't represent failure; it represents being human. We begin with good intentions, lose our way in distractions, fall into convenience, correct ourselves when something nudges our awareness, and eventually return — imperfectly but sincerely.

Millennials and Gen Z move through this loop instinctively. They don't need guilt to shift their behaviour. They need visibility, gentle reminders, and tools that meet them where they are.

The Dual Identity Advantage

What sets this generation apart is their dual identity. They understand the simplicity of the world before hyper-consumption, and they understand the convenience-driven world after it. They have lived both realities — the slow and the fast — and they carry the ability to move between them.

They are modern yet nostalgic, digital yet grounded, fast yet thoughtful. Their imperfection does not hinder them; it makes them relatable. They are aware enough to recognise wasteful habits and flexible enough to correct them. They hold the wisdom of the past and the adaptability needed for the future.

They are not a "lost generation" in the sustainability conversation. They are the bridge — linking memory with innovation, instinct with insight.

Why This Generation Can Lead the Change

When impact becomes visible, behaviour naturally follows. This generation responds to transparency, adapts quickly when things become measurable, and seeks agency over instruction. They adjust when the system makes change easy, and they lean toward choices that align with their identity as aware, informed, future-conscious individuals.

They don't resist sustainable behaviour. They simply need it presented in a way that fits the speed and structure of their lives. And with the right tools — ones that make the invisible visible — their dormant instincts awaken.

They lived sustainable childhoods.

They crafted digital adulthoods.

Now they stand at the intersection where meaningful environmental change can begin — not through perfection, but through millions of small, imperfect shifts.

The Generation Built for Imperfect Environmentalism

This chapter does not glorify Millennials and Gen Z; it recognises them. They carry the memory of low-waste living, the habits of tech-enabled convenience, and the flexibility to choose differently. They desire to align who they are with how they live.

They are imperfect — beautifully, powerfully imperfect.

And in a world where climate solutions require both memory and innovation, this generation is exactly what the planet needs.

Chapter 5:
Imperfect Environmentalism Defined

Imperfect Environmentalism is often mistaken for a gentle, individual philosophy — a softer way of saying, "Do what you can, don't overwhelm yourself." While that sentiment is partly true, it barely scratches the surface. The real meaning is far bigger, because no individual lives alone in the world. Human behaviour is woven into systems. Systems are built and maintained by businesses. Businesses respond to regulators. Regulators evolve based on public sentiment, global risk, and economic realities.

The loop is not personal.

The loop is collective.

One of the great flaws of traditional sustainability lies in how it isolates responsibility. It tells individuals to change their habits, reduce their usage, recycle more, buy less — all without acknowledging that they operate inside environments designed for convenience, not consciousness. People are asked to be perfect inside systems built for imperfection. It scolds the individual for buying plastic, but not the system that made plastic the easiest option.

Imperfect Environmentalism rejects this imbalance.

It recognises that behaviour is shared, influence is shared, and responsibility is shared. Individuals can only make the choices available to them. Businesses can only prioritize what regulators incentivize. Regulators can only act at the speed society understands. Each actor is imperfect, yet deeply connected.

This is why the loop matters — not just the loop of personal habits, but the loop of the entire ecosystem.

When Ms. Imperfect and Mr. Imperfect first discussed this, climate wasn't even the topic. They were talking about why people find change so difficult.

"It's not that people don't want to do better," she said. "It's that the world around them pulls them back into old patterns before they realise it."

Mr. Imperfect nodded. "Systems create habits. Humans adapt to systems."

This simple observation sits at the core of Imperfect Environmentalism.

---

1. The Individual Loop: Intention → Convenience → Correction → Improvement

People don't change in straight lines. They move in loops. They set positive intentions, get distracted by the pressure of daily life, fall back into convenience, correct themselves when awareness returns, and then improve — a little at a time.

This isn't human failure.

This is human behaviour.

No one on the planet lives sustainably every single day. But individuals respond strongly to visibility. When they can *see* the impact of their choices — the numbers, the comparisons, the real influence — they adjust intuitively.

Not perfectly.

But consistently enough to matter.

This loop is the first piece of imperfect environmentalism.

---

2. The Business Loop: Incentives → Pressure → Adaptation → Reinvention

Businesses also move through their own imperfect loops. Most were built in a time when consumption was celebrated, not questioned. Their systems are large, complex, and tied to short-term outcomes. Yet the landscape has changed — regulators, investors, customers, and emerging risk frameworks are demanding evolution.

Some businesses make surface-level shifts.

Others redesign entire operations.

Most are still learning that long-term survival depends on environmental intelligence.

Their loop is imperfect — but it is undeniably moving forward.

---

3. The Regulatory Loop: Awareness → Policy → Enforcement → Revision

Regulators know the urgency. They understand the science. But they must work inside political cycles, economic dependencies, and global negotiations. Policies take time to draft, more time to implement, and even more time to refine.

Regulation rarely leaps.

But each incremental step creates pressure businesses cannot ignore.

The regulatory loop may be slow and imperfect — but it is essential.

---

4. The System Loop: Design → Behaviour → Data → Redesign

Systems — financial, digital, logistical, technological — shape individual paths. People cannot recycle if infrastructure doesn't exist. They cannot choose lower-impact options if information is hidden. They cannot change behaviour if systems are designed for waste.

Systems must be redesigned for *imperfect people*, not idealized citizens who never slip. This is where environmental intelligence tools find purpose: they make the invisible visible in a world that hides impact by default.

Once visibility emerges, behaviour naturally follows.

---

5. The Consumption Loop: Desire → Purchase → Impact → Reflection

Every loop eventually converges at one point: consumption.

Individuals choose based on behaviour.

Businesses choose based on incentives.

Regulators choose based on risk.

Systems choose based on design.

All these choices result in environmental impact.

Imperfect Environmentalism understands that this loop cannot be changed through guilt — only through awareness, thoughtful design, and aligned incentives. Pressure alone cannot shift consumption. Insight can.

Why Imperfect Environmentalism Works

Imperfect Environmentalism is not a diluted form of sustainability.

It is a more realistic one.

It accepts that people will forget.

Businesses will slip.

Regulators will delay.

Systems will misalign.

And instead of demanding perfection from any one part of the ecosystem, it builds a philosophy that works *because* of the imperfection.

It doesn't demonize the loop.

It designs with the loop.

The goal is not transformation through force.

It is transformation through momentum.

When individuals shift their choices, businesses respond.

When businesses adapt, systems evolve.

When systems evolve, regulators accelerate.

When regulators accelerate, the whole loop becomes smarter.

Not perfect — but smarter.

Not flawless — but functional.

Not instant — but inevitable.

The True Meaning of Imperfect Environmentalism

Imperfect Environmentalism is the belief that climate responsibility must be shared — intelligently, realistically, and collectively.

A world where progress matters more than perfection.

A world where environmental action is built into the daily structure of life.

A world where systems support imperfect humans instead of punishing them.

A world where small shifts accumulate into large impacts because the entire loop is aligned.

Once you understand this, the next question becomes clearer:

How do we guide imperfect behaviour?

How do we create visibility in a world built on invisible impact?

How do we understand the imperfect consumer, and the money mindset shaping the world we live in?

Answering these questions is what leads us directly into the heart of the next chapter — not through force, not through moral pressure, but through deep understanding.

Imperfect Environmentalism is not about fixing people.

It is about understanding them well enough to guide the behaviour they already have.

Part II

The Problem We Couldn't Unsee

(Money, Mindset & Modern Consumption)

Chapter 6:

The Imperfect Consumer in an Imperfect System

The more Ms. Imperfect and Mr. Imperfect observed the world, the clearer it became that environmental problems were never the fault of one player, one decision-maker, or one behaviour. Not the consumer alone. Not businesses alone. Not governments alone. Every layer of society carried its own limits, pressures, contradictions, and imperfections.

What troubled them most wasn't that people were failing —

it was that people were being asked to succeed inside structures designed to make failure easier than success.

This was the problem they couldn't unsee.

---

1. The Imperfect Consumer

Modern consumption is a perfect storm of convenience, invisibility, and emotional fatigue. People wake up balancing deadlines, responsibilities, financial pressure, family, stress — and in the middle of this overwhelm, the world around them has made consumption effortless.

One tap delivers groceries.

A few clicks bring home outfits.

A sale notification changes an entire day's behaviour.

Almost nothing requires planning.

Even less requires awareness.

Consumers aren't unwilling to live sustainably –

they are exhausted.

They don't ignore the environment; they simply don't *see* the consequences. A food-delivery app never shows the emissions behind delivery bikes, cold-chain logistics, and packaging. A flight ticket displays timing and price, not atmospheric cost. Even a shampoo bottle reveals nothing about its end-of-life footprint.

Invisibility shapes behaviour far more effectively than intention ever can.

One evening, Ms. Imperfect held up a plastic bag she had accepted without thinking.

"Most people never chose this," she said quietly. "It was chosen for them."

Mr. Imperfect nodded. He had spent years watching consumers blamed for problems they didn't create. The system made the wrong thing easy and the right thing difficult.

How could imperfect people behave perfectly inside imperfect design?

Consumers aren't the problem.

They are the symptom of a system that hides the cost of convenience.

---

2. The Imperfect Business

Businesses live inside their own loop of limitations. They don't wake up intending to harm the planet; they wake up responding to incentives. For decades, the world rewarded companies for speed, scale, low cost, and constant growth. Markets celebrated volume, not virtue. Consumers demanded discounts. Investors demanded quarterly performance. Supply chains were engineered for efficiency, not responsibility.

When businesses attempt to act sustainably, they encounter contradictions everywhere. Greener raw materials are more expensive. Cleaner energy requires upfront investment. Ethical procurement slows production. Sustainable packaging increases pricing — and most consumers still hesitate to pay more.

So, businesses try, adjust, compromise, and then slip back into old patterns.

And then came the global imbalance triggered by the **Paris Agreement**.

The Agreement — signed in 2015 — pledged the world to limit warming to "well below 2°C." Every country committed. But not every country started from the same position.

Developed nations had already industrialised, built infrastructure, accumulated capital, and built public pressure for environmental action. They could enforce strict compliance quickly.

Developing nations, however, were still building — cities, industries, infrastructure, livelihoods. Their emissions were tied not to luxury but to growth and survival. They needed to expand before they could reduce.

This mismatch created deep tensions:

- A European exporter must comply with strict sustainability rules immediately.
- An Indian or Indonesian supplier struggles because cleaner infrastructure is costly.
- Banks financing projects must meet global climate norms, even if domestic systems lag behind.
- A small African manufacturer must achieve standards it had no resources to plan for.

Businesses found themselves caught between two worlds:

one demanding rapid compliance, another still fighting for equitable development time.

The result?

Short-term compliance became the norm — certificates, reports, offsets — not out of dishonesty, but out of survival.

Keeping the business alive often felt more urgent than redesigning the future.

---

3. The Imperfect Regulator

Regulators operate inside one of the most complex loops in the ecosystem. They must balance climate urgency with political realities, economic growth with social stability, global commitments with national capability.

A policy that is too strict can cripple industries.

A policy that is too lenient can fail the planet.

Policies take years to design, negotiate, approve, and implement. They require coordination across ministries, sectors, regions, and sometimes entire continents. Even once policies are passed, enforcement varies — infrastructure may be weak, budgets limited, or public readiness too low.

Regulators do not resist environmental progress;

they manage the friction of progress.

Their imperfection is not failure —

it is the weight of governing a world that is transforming faster than institutions can adapt.

---

4. The Imperfect System

The founders' most profound realisation came when they understood that the **system itself** was never designed for sustainability.

Cities, power grids, factories, packaging norms, transportation networks, waste management — most of these were built in the 20th century, an era obsessed with efficiency, affordability, and growth. Climate impact was not a metric. It wasn't even a thought.

We inherited a world engineered for expansion, not preservation.

Expecting perfect sustainable behaviour inside outdated infrastructure is like trying to run modern software on an obsolete operating system — the intention is strong, but the architecture is incompatible.

Systems change slowly because rebuilding them requires imagination, capital, political will, and time. Yet while systems evolve inch by inch, consumers and businesses are expected to leap.

This is the tension the founders could not ignore.

---

5. The Loop the Founders Couldn't Ignore

Once Ms. Imperfect and Mr. Imperfect saw the full picture — the imperfect consumer, the imperfect business, the imperfect regulator, and the imperfect system — they realised something important:

It was impossible to isolate a villain.

Every layer of society was doing the best it could with the visibility it had:

Consumers acted on convenience because impact was invisible.

Businesses acted on incentives because markets demanded it.

Regulators acted on global commitments because the climate required it.

Systems acted on historical design because rebuilding takes decades.

Everyone imperfect.

Everyone trying.

Everyone limited by what they could see.

One night, Ms. Imperfect said softly, "People want to do better. They just don't know how to do better in the world they've inherited."

Mr. Imperfect added gently, "And businesses want to improve too — but they're following signals that were never designed for sustainability."

In that moment, the pieces aligned.

Not as a solution, but as a spark.

The world didn't need guilt.

It needed guidance.

It didn't need perfect systems.

It needed visible systems.

It didn't need perfect people.

It needed imperfect people with better information.

And from that spark arose the question that would define everything that followed:

If the world is imperfect at every level,

how can this imperfect duo build something

that helps everyone see more clearly?

Chapter 7:

The Imperfect Duo

They did not begin as Business Partners.

They began as two people living their separate, imperfect lives — each shaped by different worlds, different careers, different instincts, yet drawn toward similar questions they didn't yet know how to articulate.

Ms. Imperfect came from decades of understanding human behaviour.

She had spent her life decoding why people buy, what influences them, what triggers action and what numbs it. Her work in advertising and marketing had taught her a paradox she could never ignore:

she was exceptionally good at driving consumption — even in people who didn't truly need what they were buying.

And that troubled her.

She believed in sustainability long before it became a boardroom word, yet she watched how campaigns, trends, flash sales, and psychological nudges shaped patterns of overconsumption. She saw how behaviour could be engineered — how desires could be created, accelerated, and rewarded.

Her discomfort grew quietly, like a background hum she couldn't switch off.

By the time the world entered the pre-COVID digital boom, she knew she needed to understand something deeper — not just why people consume, but why they struggle to stop.

So, she stepped into finance and fintech.

Because if money drives behaviour, then the world of finance is where you truly learn the **nature of human decision-making**.

Fintech in India was exploding.

UPI was rewriting transaction behaviour.

Trading apps were reshaping investment culture.

And Ms. Imperfect saw clearly:

if people can be nudged into financial habits,

they can be nudged into environmental ones.

On the other side of this story lived Mr. Imperfect.

A creator.

A builder.

A product thinker with an instinct for solving invisible problems through elegant, tech-first systems.

He wasn't a marketer; he was a maker — the kind who sees a gap and immediately begins designing a solution in his head. As a Certified Financial Planner and founder of his own fintech product, he understood the engine behind money better than most:

how transactions behave,

how systems process choices,

how data reveals patterns,

and how products can guide behaviour without force.

Where Ms. Imperfect studied human psychology,

Mr. Imperfect studied human patterns.

And though they didn't know it yet,

they were two halves of the same unanswered question.

When Their Worlds Crossed

They first connected online in 2019 — a period when the world was rapidly shifting, and fintech was evolving even faster. What began as a conversation about product strategy slowly drifted into deeper discussions about the world around them.

They talked about finance, markets, consumer psychology, product adoption…

and then, unexpectedly, the conversation shifted to sustainability.

Not the textbook kind —

but the real kind, the behavioural kind.

How people were consuming more but understanding less.

How money shaped every decision but hid every consequence.

How the world celebrated convenience without revealing its cost.

And then came that one conversation — the one Ms. Imperfect still calls their "Apple Moment."

A colleague at work had bought the newest iPhone and proudly called it a "depreciating piece of jewellery."

They laughed at the phrase, but the insight beneath it was sharp.

Ms. Imperfect pointed out that while the iPhone depreciates in *financial* value the moment it's unboxed, it also represents something much bigger in the climate story: a device designed with a sustainability architecture far ahead of its competitors — carbon-neutral manufacturing efforts, recycling programs, reduced plastic packaging.

Mr. Imperfect expanded the thought:

Apple wasn't just selling a device.

It was building an ecosystem — a financial system, a technological system, and a sustainability system tied together.

They realised something profound:

the world's most influential brands were already making climate action invisible, unproblematic, and integrated... but most people had no idea.

That conversation sat with them for days.

The Spark That Wouldn't Leave

By 2022, they both realised the world is really small. They both ended up in the same company.

Mr. Imperfect has made a successful exit from his last venture and was called by the founders as consultant and Ms. Imperfect was leading the marketing bandwagon of this upcoming behavioural fintech product.

Their friendship deepened, and so did their conversations.

One day, Mr. Imperfect was working on a survey for a new product — an idea around what he called "Banking 3.0," a reimagined system that could include sustainability as a core feature. He sent the survey to Ms. Imperfect, almost casually.

She read it, stood up from her desk, walked straight to him, and asked:

"What exactly are you trying to build?"

He smiled, as if she had asked the exact question he had been waiting for.

"I'm thinking about a system where money, behaviour, and impact speak to each other. Not separately — but in one loop."

She paused.

"Do you mean a banking system that makes climate action visible in daily life? That shows impact the way credit scores show financial behaviour?"

He nodded.

"Why should sustainable behaviour be the only thing the world can't see?"

It was the conversation that changed everything.

From Curiosity to Creation

They began sending surveys to their networks —

IIM alumni, ISB alumni, industry friends, professionals in finance and sustainability.

The results surprised them.

People said they cared.

People said they would pay.

People said they wanted tools to understand their impact.

But when asked for actual data —

their electricity usage, fuel consumption, waste habits, shopping patterns —

almost no one wanted to share it.

Not because they were unwilling.

Because it was *too much work.*

Sustainability required more effort than most people had the emotional or mental bandwidth for.

That's when Ms. Imperfect said something that would define their journey:

"People aren't avoiding responsibility.

They're avoiding overwhelm."

They realised the problem wasn't intention —

it was design.

Sustainability tools were too manual, too complicated, too demanding.

People didn't need moral pressure.

They needed simplicity.

And money — the one thing already recorded, measured, tracked, and analysed —

held the key.

The Decision That Changed Their Lives

In the middle of this growing clarity, they had a personal moment of truth.

Both admitted they were not perfectly "green" either.

They weren't vegan.

They weren't zero-waste.

They weren't plastic-free.

They were human.

And that honesty connected them to the people they wanted to help.

They didn't want to build a system for perfect environmentalists.

They wanted to build a system for imperfect ones — people like themselves.

Within weeks, the decision was made.

They resigned from their jobs.

They pooled their savings.

They created their first prototypes.

And they named their dream:

Myplan8 —

because the planet cannot have just one plan.

It needs an infinite loop of actions,

driven by people who try, fail, correct, and try again.

The number eight became a symbol —

an infinity loop

and a reminder that sustainability is a continuous journey,

not a finish line.

Two Imperfect People, One Shared Vision

They didn't begin as founders.

They became founders because they couldn't unsee what they had seen.

They didn't begin with a perfect plan.

They began with imperfect questions.

And together, they would build something the world urgently needed:

a way for everyday transactions to reveal their hidden impact,

a way for the invisible to become visible,

a way for imperfect people to take meaningful steps.

Not through guilt.

Not through pressure.

But through design, intelligence, and awareness.

Two imperfect minds.

One shared purpose.

The journey — the real journey — had only just begun.

Chapter 8:

The Power of Money in Climate Action

Money has always influenced human behaviour — quietly, consistently, almost invisibly. Not because people worship it, but because everything they touch, use, consume, build, or dream flows through money before it becomes reality. In today's world, almost nothing moves without a transaction. And this truth is what began to crystallize for Ms. Imperfect and Mr. Imperfect once Myplan8® was born.

They had mapped the imperfect loops — the consumer, the business, the regulator, the system. Yet something deeper was still missing. Something universal. Something that could connect every loop without demanding perfection from any of them. Something understood by every individual, every business, every institution.

It wasn't policy.

It wasn't awareness.

It wasn't guilt.

It wasn't reporting frameworks.

It wasn't even sustainability knowledge.

It was money.

Not just physical currency — but **the financial trail of human life**.

Every tap, swipe, bill payment, payroll cycle, vendor invoice, tax deduction, subscription, order confirmation — every one of these left a footprint not only on the planet, but inside a ledger.

A ledger that was already complete.

Already precise.

Already trusted.

Already unavoidable.

Money had quietly been doing the job sustainability tools struggled with — capturing patterns, day after day, without needing anyone to remember anything.

But before this realization arrived, something else opened their eyes.

A Survey That Revealed the Gap

The founders sent a simple survey to their IIM and ISB alumni networks — people from finance, technology, consulting, and management backgrounds.

The first question was straightforward:

"Would you pay for a product that helps you reduce your environmental impact?"

Almost everyone said *yes*.

The enthusiasm was almost unanimous.

But the follow-up question changed everything:

"Do you know what your carbon footprint even is?"

Most people admitted they had absolutely no idea.

Not because they didn't care —

but because they didn't understand the language.

So, the founders explored the world of carbon footprint calculators — the globally accepted tools designed to measure impact.

From the outside, these calculators appeared robust.

Scientific.

Accurate.

Comprehensive.

But the moment they tried using them, reality hit.

"How many units of electricity do you use each month?"

"What is your vehicle's average fuel consumption?"

"How many litres per mile does your car burn?"

"How many flights did you take last year?"

"What's your weekly breakdown of dairy, vegetables, poultry, red meat?"

"How often do you order online?"

"What appliances do you own and what are their wattages?"

On and on it went — a never-ending interrogation.

Ms. Imperfect exhaled sharply.

"This is a full-time job," she muttered.

Mr. Imperfect didn't look up from the screen.

"No one in the world will fill this."

They weren't wrong.

The science was correct — but the method was unrealistic.

People don't know their wattages.

They don't track their yearly flights.

They don't weigh their food habits.

They don't record their consumption in categories.

Sustainability required more memory and manual effort than real life allows.

And then, ironically, the founders noticed something important:

People may not remember their carbon data —

but they remember **every rupee (or dollar) they spend**.

Receipts in email.

Bank statements.

Order histories.

Card bills.

UPI logs.

App notifications.

Salary credits.

Utility payments.

Money was already doing the tracking that sustainability tools were begging people to do manually.

Every purchase was a pattern.

Every bill was a footprint.

Every payment was a behavioural signal.

Every transaction was a story.

The world did not suffer from a lack of data.

It suffered from data hidden in the wrong place.

The Moment the Puzzle Clicked

Ms. Imperfect said quietly, "It's strange — the world is drowning in sustainability reports, yet no one knows their own footprint."

Mr. Imperfect smiled slightly.

"But everyone knows their bank statement.

Everyone knows their bills.

Everyone knows every dime they spend."

And suddenly, the answer became obvious.

Everything carbon calculators tried to extract manually

was already captured automatically in the financial trail.

Money never lies.

Money never forgets.

Money doesn't need to be collected.

Money doesn't need to be estimated.

Money is an honest mirror of behaviour.

If money is the record of consumption,

then money can also be the record of impact.

The question was no longer:

"How do we collect data?"

It became:

"How do we translate data?"

How do we make the invisible visible?

How do we reveal impact through the currency people already understand?

How do we allow money — the world's most universal behavioural tool —

to become the world's most intuitive climate tool?

They didn't yet know how the system would work.

They had no algorithms, no technology stack, no scoring model, no architecture.

But they had clarity.

This moment — simple, quiet, but seismic — marked the turning point.

For the first time, they could see a pathway where sustainability didn't require extra effort, extra knowledge, extra motivation, or extra memory.

A path where:

Money becomes the language of climate action.

Transactions become touchpoints.

Impact becomes visible.

Behaviour shifts naturally.

A world where the unseen becomes seen.

And this realization set the foundation for everything they would build next.

Part III

The World We Can Build

Chapter 9

Making the Invisible Visible

Once they realised that money could reveal what people never remembered, a more difficult question emerged – one that would define the next phase of their thinking:

If money can tell the story,

how do you *tell* the story in a way the human mind instantly understands?

This was not a technical problem.

It was a psychological one.

Because the moment they stepped into the world of emissions, they discovered something no one ever warns you about: **the language of sustainability fights against human instinct.**

"Net zero" sounds good, yet humans have never been conditioned to celebrate zero.

"Carbon negative" is even better for the planet, but the word "negative" feels like failure.

"Carbon positive" is harmful, yet the word "positive" feels uplifting.

Nothing aligned.

Not with intuition.

Not with behaviour.

Not with emotion.

One afternoon, Ms. Imperfect joked, "Even if someone is doing everything right, telling them they're 'negative' will make them miserable."

It was funny — until they realised, she was right.

Humans are psychologically wired to respond to:

- numbers that rise,
- benchmarks that compare,
- progress indicators that reward,
- and metrics that show improvement — not reduction.

Environmental metrics do the opposite.

They ask people to *reduce*, to aim for *less*, to find motivation in shrinking numbers.

But nothing in modern life trains the mind to celebrate "less."

Not performance.

Not finances.

Not ambition.

Mr. Imperfect put it plainly:

"The numbers in sustainability argue with the human mind."

That was the intersection they stood at:

Money could translate consumption into emissions —

but emissions still needed *translation* for the human brain.

The Problem of Meaning

They tested this insight with friends, colleagues, and alumni. The patterns were identical.

"Your morning coffee emitted 0.4 kg of CO_2e."

Confusion.

No emotional response. No understanding.

"Your day emitted 12 kg of CO_2e."

The same question, every time:

"Is that okay? Is that too much? Compared to what?"

People weren't resisting climate understanding.

They simply lacked a **reference point** — a way to understand whether a number was good, bad, or somewhere in the middle.

Businesses struggled just as much.

A person thinks in habits.

A business thinks in frameworks.

But both were blind when it came to interpreting emissions meaningfully.

The data existed, but **the meaning was missing**.

And without meaning, awareness cannot become action.

Scores: The Language Humans Already Understand

One evening, while discussing this frustration, Ms. Imperfect said, "In fintech, people understand credit scores instantly. They don't know the formulas — they just know what the score *means*."

Mr. Imperfect nodded. "Same with risk scores, compliance scores, behavioural scores. No one memorises them. People understand them because a score tells a story."

The truth settled between them.

Scores simplify complexity.

Scores make behaviour visible.

Scores turn invisible patterns into emotional meaning.

Scores are universal — used by individuals, businesses, institutions, and regulators alike.

The world already understands scores.

They don't question them.

They don't fear them.

They trust them.

Suddenly, the path forward became clear:

They didn't need more data.

They didn't need more awareness.

They didn't need more jargon.

They needed a **single, unified way to express environmental behaviour in a language humans already speak.**

For individuals, it would show whether daily choices were good, bad, or in between.

For businesses, it would reveal responsibility, regulatory readiness, operational impact, and financial risk.

One language.

Two audiences.

One interpretation engine.

A bridge between the emotional world of people

and the structural world of companies.

Money → Emission → **Meaning**

That was the chain that could finally make the invisible visible.

The Spark of a New Wheel

This wasn't a tool yet.

This wasn't a product.

This wasn't a framework.

It was a **way of thinking** — a wheel the sustainability world had never built before.

A simple idea that held enormous potential:

If the world already understands scores,

why not use a score to help the world understand its impact?

It would take months to shape,

years to refine,

and a lifetime to scale.

But the foundation had been laid.

This was not a conclusion.

This was the beginning.

The beginning of inventing something the world of climate action had never seen —

a way to turn invisible emissions into visible meaning

for people, for businesses, and for every imperfect mind trying to do better.

Chapter 10:

Environmental Quotient — The Green Scoring System

They didn't realise it at first. Not in the moment. Not even in the week that followed. But the idea arrived the way most world-changing insights do—quietly. Not with fireworks or fanfare, but with the subtle force of truth settling into place. It was like

Archimedes stepping into a bath and suddenly understanding buoyancy;

Like Newton watching an apple fall and wondering why it didn't drift sideways;

Like Einstein questioning why time should remain still when everything else moved.

The moment when something that had always been there finally becomes visible.

For Ms. Imperfect and Mr. Imperfect, that moment came when they realised that money could make the invisible visible—but visibility alone wasn't enough.

Sustainability wasn't a report or a checklist; it was a journey. And every journey, whether across a city or across a lifetime, needs the same four instruments:

A **map** to understand the destination,

A **compass** to point toward the right direction,

A **GPS** to guide through changing paths, and

A **speedometer** to show progress.

She said it softly that night, but the words felt heavier than everything they had seen in their professional lives: “People don’t know where they are. Businesses don’t know where they’re going. The world doesn’t have a compass.”

He nodded, because he had felt it too. “A journey without navigation,” he murmured, “is just wandering.” And sustainability, for decades, had been wandering.

The Maze of Tools Without a Dashboard

Imagine being told to drive from one end of a country to another without knowing the distance, the route, the direction, the terrain, or the detours. Intention would collapse under confusion. This was the world in 2021–2022.

Consumers wanted to act, businesses wanted to improve, governments wanted reduction, regulators wanted credibility, banks wanted clarity—yet no one had a navigation system. Frameworks existed, yes, but frameworks are not maps. They tell you what to measure, not how to move. They tell you what is mandatory, not how to improve. They tell you what went wrong, not what you should do next. Everyone was trying—but no one was guided.

Businesses across the world were trying harder than ever. Apple was redesigning materials and committing to a carbon-neutral supply chain. IKEA was rebuilding operations around circularity. Patagonia was advising customers not to buy unless necessary.

The European Union introduced the Digital Product Passport, forcing companies to reveal the complete environmental story of every product. The world was shifting. And yet businesses were drowning in a sea of frameworks:

Product life-cycle assessments,

GHG Protocol scopes,

DEFRA factors,

ESG disclosures,

SDGs,

Investor expectations, climate risk models, supplier emissions, and local environmental laws.

Each tool was valuable—yet none spoke to another. It was a maze of brilliance without a map.

One afternoon, after hours of dissecting regulatory PDFs, Mr. Imperfect leaned back and said, "The world has the instruments, but not the dashboard." Ms. Imperfect replied, "We don't need new frameworks. We need a universal interpreter."

The world didn't lack science; it lacked synthesis. It lacked a way to translate scattered truths into a single, coherent guidance system.

A Language People Could Finally Understand

People were no different. If businesses were lost technically, individuals were lost emotionally. Sustainability spoke in a language that contradicted human instincts. Positive meant bad; negative meant good; zero meant achievement.

Reducing numbers felt like losing. Increasing numbers felt like winning. And yet climate action required the opposite. Humans are not designed to celebrate negative numbers or glorify reduction. People weren't unwilling—they were simply unaligned with the language.

They understood calories on packages, credit scores on loans, customer ratings on apps, fitness scores on watches. Because scores compress complexity into clarity. Scores make people feel oriented. Scores motivate improvement. Scores connect emotionally. A score is a mirror that does not punish—it guides.

And there—right there—was the moment when emotional truth and technical truth collided. Product life-cycle assessment (LCA), the scientific process of measuring emissions across a product's entire life, became the foundation. Money trails revealed what people and businesses truly consumed. AI created the intelligence required to interpret patterns across millions of actions.

Global frameworks—UNFCCC, GHG Protocol, DEFRA, SDGs, ESG, and the Digital Product Passport—offered structure and credibility. Behavioural science translated this complexity into a simple, intuitive, emotionally meaningful metric. For the first time, the architecture was visible: lifecycle science as the base; money as the behavioural record; AI as the brain; global frameworks as the skeleton; and a score as the emotional language. A complete wheel.

The Architecture Was Already in the World — Just Unassembled

"We're not building a tool," Mr. Imperfect said one evening, unable to hide the awe in his voice. "We're building a brain."

"And a language," she added.

"And a compass. A map. A GPS. A speedometer."

"It's a navigation system," he concluded. "For the world."

Carbon calculators existed, but felt academic. Certifications existed but were binary. Scores existed but were limited to finances or health. Patagonia had moral clarity, IKEA had vision, Apple had lifecycle mastery, and the EU had regulatory courage. But no one had woven all of it into a single navigation system. No one had built a real-time environmental GPS that could guide both individuals and businesses.

The Green People Score — Behaviour Meets Clarity

The Green People Score emerged first—an emotional mirror for daily life. Ms. Imperfect struggled for months to explain it simply.

Then one day she said, "Think of what a credit score does for your financial handling. It tells you if you're managing money well or drifting off track." The analogy unlocked everything. "Then the Green People Score," she continued, "is your **moral compass** for how your money impacts the environment."

It showed people how their lifestyle choices—mobility, food, convenience, spending—shaped their environmental behaviour. And just like a credit score shows the path to improve financially, the Green People Score showed the **destination** for becoming more climate-conscious and the **route** to get there. It never judged—it guided.

The Green Business Score — The First True Environmental Maturity Model

The personal score was behavioural.

The business score needed to be structural.

The Green Business Score needed a different structure.

Mr. Imperfect explained it simply: "If credit ratings help businesses understand their financial risk, then the Green Business Score helps them understand their **environmental maturity**."

It unified: governance readiness, lifecycle integration, ESG alignment, SDG progress, climate financial risk, supply chain emissions, and regulatory preparedness.

It wasn't a badge. It was a compass—one that finally pointed north.

The Meeting That Tested Everything — and Changed Everything

With both scores finally taking shape, they realised they weren't just creating metrics—they were creating a universal language. A system that could be used by banks to guide climate finance, by regulators to establish clarity, by businesses to track maturity, and by individuals to understand their daily behaviour.

But they also knew that every invention carries blind spots its creators cannot see. They needed someone who would question it with precision. Someone who would poke holes without hesitation. Someone who would not be impressed—just honest. So, they called their mentor. And he, in turn, sent them to someone whose opinion carried weight in the heart of India's financial world.

This unexpectedly in their own journey turned out to be one of major turning point, they met at a lush cricket club in the heart of Mumbai's Bandra-Kurla Complex — the centre of corporate India.

Their mentor had arranged a meeting with someone renowned for his sharp mind and sharper critiques. "If anyone can break your idea," he said, "it's him." The founders walked into the quiet wooden interiors overlooking manicured lawns and the corporate towers of Bandra-Kurla Complex—Mumbai's hard, glittering core of finance, regulation, and power.

They presented everything: the money-emission link, the behavioural logic, the emotional interpretation, the need for a scoring system, and the framework connecting global science with personal and corporate habits. They expected him to challenge them.

They *wanted* him to challenge them. But he loved the idea. He nodded thoughtfully. He spoke about his children learning sustainability in school. He talked about how his parents lived simply and sustainably without ever naming it. He praised the clarity they had created.

And then the food arrived.

He had ordered far more than he could finish. When the waiter packed the leftovers in a plastic container wrapped in a paper bag, he waved his hand. "Just throw it away."

Ms. Imperfect didn't let the moment pass. She said gently, "Sir, that leftover food will release methane—far more potent than CO_2. And the plastic container, even this paper bag, all have lifecycle emissions too. You just said you are one of the most sustainable people you know. This one moment," she added softly, "is exactly why people need guidance. Not guilt—visibility."

He froze—not defensively, but reflectively. Something shifted.

That night he called them.

"I want to invest," he said simply.

"And I want you to protect this idea. Patent everything. The methodology, the system, the language. This is not a small solution. This is a global system."

Before ending the call, he asked them one question:

"What do you want to become?"

They looked at each other.

And said the truth aloud for the first time:

"A green bank… but that would limit us."

He replied, "Then don't be a bank. Become the engine every bank uses."

And that became the defining pivot.

Becoming a bank would have bound them to geography. Becoming an engine liberated them across continents. A bank influences customers; an engine influences ecosystems.

Protecting a Global Method, Not a Product

A bank speaks to a city; an engine speaks to a world. The decision was clear: they would not become a bank—they would become the universal intelligence behind banks, regulators, businesses, and communities.

When the architecture finally stood whole—map, compass, GPS, speedometer, lifecycle science, money trails, AI, global frameworks, and the twin scoring system—they fell silent. Not out of pride, but out of responsibility.

"This isn't just ours," she said.

"It belongs to the world," he replied.

"And that is exactly why it must be protected."

So, they protected not the code or visuals, but the method, the philosophy, the wheel itself—the Environmental Quotient. Not to gatekeep it, but to safeguard its integrity.

In the end, what they had built was not a feature or an app or a rating. It was a **language**. A navigation system for an imperfect world. A way for people and businesses to finally say, "We know where we are. We know where we need to go. And now, we finally know how to get there."

Chapter 11:

Perfection in Small Actions

Most revolutions don't begin with declarations. They begin with small choices—tiny, almost forgettable decisions that shape who we become. Ms. Imperfect often said, "People look for the dramatic gesture, but the planet is healed by the quiet ones." And Mr. Imperfect would nod, amused by how simple and profound that sounded. "It's the small actions we repeat," he said once, "that change the slope of the future."

By the time they shaped the Environmental Quotient into the Green People Score and the Green Business Score, they had already realised something fundamental: sustainability is not driven by big sacrifices but by **small, imperfect behaviours made visible and meaningful**. The scoring system was not built to worship perfection; it was built to guide everyday people and everyday businesses. It was designed to awaken the unconscious part of human behaviour—the part that is honest, messy, habitual, deeply human.

They both understood that the world didn't lack good intentions; it lacked visibility. In behavioural science, people don't change when they are lectured. They change when they can *see* themselves. That was the backbone of this chapter: the visibility of small actions.

What a Flight Really Means

Think of a flight. A simple, everyday act of life. People fly because life takes them places—jobs, responsibilities, families, dreams, loves, losses. Flying isn't evil; it's human. But for decades, no airline showed passengers what those flights meant environmentally.

"It's strange," Ms. Imperfect murmured one afternoon, looking at a ticket receipt, "we know exactly how much the ticket cost, but no one tells us the cost to the planet."

Mr. Imperfect leaned back, thoughtful. "Money always shows the transaction. But the atmosphere never sends a bill."

Some airlines offered symbolic gestures—₹3 for "green offsets," avoid-the-bottle nudges. But there was no real disclosure, no alternatives, no comparisons. People weren't guided—they were guessing.

Europe approached this differently. France, Germany, Italy, and Scandinavia began showing rail vs. flight emissions right at the booking interface. Sweden's "flygskam" movement shifted thousands to trains. France even banned certain domestic flights. People didn't change because they were told to—they changed because the alternative was **visible**.

"That's all people need," she whispered. "Just to see."

"And when they see," he replied, "they recalibrate."

That is why the Green People Score existed—not to ban flights but to guide choices. Sustainability wasn't punishment. It was partnership.

Inside a Business, Small Actions Echo Even Louder

Inside businesses, small actions amplified even more. Most organisations didn't realise their environmental behaviour was already recorded in thousands of data points—ERP logs, HRMS systems, vendor invoices, electricity meters, employee travel, procurement sheets.

"Look at this," Mr. Imperfect once said, pointing at a dataset from a mid-sized company. "They've unknowingly documented their climate story for a decade."

Every AC cycle, every courier, every unneeded printout, every unused meeting room, every leftover lunch—each action was tiny, but together, they shaped an entire sustainability narrative.

Countries across the world were proving this. Singaporean banks reduced paper-heavy onboarding and optimised branch cooling systems. Japan digitised entire employee expense workflows. The Nordics redesigned offices around cycle-to-work culture. The UK introduced low-waste office certifications. Canada normalised sustainability training.

These weren't big overhauls—they were thousands of tiny shifts.

During one such discussion, Ms. Imperfect said,

"You know how companies brag about being a Great Place to Work?"

He nodded.

"But what about being a *Green Place to Work*?"

He smiled. "A place where business scores and people scores rise together."

She replied softly, "A place where everyone knows every small action matters."

It was never about perfection.

It was about pattern. And behaviour. And culture.

Atomic Habits and the Mathematics of Smallness

People had already embraced this idea in other parts of life. *Atomic Habits* taught a generation that small routines compound into big outcomes. The founders saw it reflected everywhere.

"Climate action is just atomic habits applied to the planet," Mr. Imperfect said during one evening walk.

"And the scoring system is the mirror," she answered.

"A mirror that shows people the shape of their habits."

Banking and the Quiet Climate Revolution

When they studied banks, the irony fascinated them: banks quietly shaped billions of decisions yet rarely examined their own small operational behaviours. Branch cooling, ATM power draw, courier cycles, cash logistics, printed passbooks, cheque books—none of these were malicious, just outdated.

Digital banking, however, quietly reimagined everything.

Singapore's fintech simplified onboarding.

Japan reduced cash usage dramatically.

The Nordics moved almost entirely to contactless payments.

European neobanks eliminated physical statements.

The UK normalised app-only banks.

And then there was an Indian example they both loved—one that felt small but profound.

A few years earlier, Indian banks like HDFC, ICICI, and SBI had started showing a simple message at ATMs:

"Skip the paper slip. Save a tree."

Later, some even displayed:

"You saved ₹X by skipping the slip this month."

It was tiny.

Barely a nudge.

Yet millions started pressing **"No."**

Paper was saved.

Costs dropped.

Behaviour shifted.

"That's the thing about small actions," Ms. Imperfect said. "They hide their power."

"And then they bloom quietly," he added.

Watching this shift live taught the founders something crucial. If one tiny ATM choice could change behaviour at national scale, then digital journeys across banking could do the same. Because they wanted to become an **engine for banks**, not a bank themselves, they realised they could help financial institutions offer hundreds of such small alternatives—paperless onboarding, digital KYC, virtual cards, online servicing—each journey quietly saving grams, then kilograms, then tonnes of emissions.

"It's not digital versus physical," Mr. Imperfect said. "It's digital unlocking the hidden savings already waiting inside a bank."

"And showing them," she added, "how every journey has a carbon fingerprint—and a carbon alternative."

Manual First — Because Humans Are the Truth

Before even thinking of starting automation, the founders wanted raw, unfiltered behaviour because behaviour mattered the most in this engine.

"Let's see how people reflect when nothing calculates for them," Ms. Imperfect said.

"And let's learn from their honesty," he replied.

They launched the manual version quietly—through alumni circles, word of mouth, community groups, and personal networks. They expected a few hundred early users.

Instead, **over 40,000+ people** participated.

Students, professionals, homemakers, bankers, teachers, retirees.

From India, Southeast Asia, the Middle East, Europe, and North America.

They wrote things like:

"I didn't realise food waste mattered."

"I didn't know deliveries increased my footprint."

"I never connected flights to anything except cost."

"My commute shocked me."

These responses became a living behavioural case study—

a natural proof that people were ready for climate awareness if guided gently.

"And if this is what happens manually," Ms. Imperfect said one night,

"imagine what happens when intelligence helps them daily."

Mr. Imperfect whispered,

"That's the future, isn't it?

A world guided softly by intelligence."

Small Imperfections, Large Futures

The more they observed, the clearer it became:

The planet will not be saved by perfect people.

It will be saved by imperfect people making millions of imperfect choices consistently.

A chosen train.

A skipped paper slip.

A smaller cafeteria portion.

A shared ride.

A mindful supplier.

A digital workflow.

A conscious meal.

A reduced waste bin.

A greener branch.

A thoughtful commute.

A lifted business score.

A lifted people score.

Each action was tiny.

Each action was human.

Each action was imperfect.

Each action was powerful.

Sustainability wasn't a grand vision.

It was a mosaic of tiny decisions—

guided by clarity,

supported by intelligence,

and multiplied across millions.

As the founders looked ahead, they felt the pull of the next chapter—not just sustainability, but consciousness.

Not just visibility, but intelligence.

They were stepping into a world where the smallest actions would be guided by something wiser, quieter, sharper—

a climate intelligence layer

designed for an imperfect world.

And that, finally, was the beginning of becoming climate-smart.

Part IV

Intelligence, Banking, Businesses & The Changing World

Chapter 12:

Becoming Climate-Smart: The Role Of AI In A Warming World

There was a time, not long ago, when the world seemed to believe that technology alone could save everything. Artificial intelligence became the new magic word — whispered in boardrooms, shouted in investor meetings, stamped on pitch decks like a seal of approval. The founders heard the same questions everywhere they went: *"Is this AI? What model are you using? Is it predictive? Is it generative?"*

Ms. Imperfect would gently smile — the patient smile of someone who understood that excitement and confusion often speak in the same tone. "AI is part of it," she would say softly, "but intelligence is bigger than algorithms." Mr. Imperfect would add, "Artificial intelligence processes the world as it is. Assisted intelligence helps us understand who we are in that world."

Somewhere in these conversations, they had jokingly coined a phrase — *AI²* — artificial plus assisted intelligence. It wasn't a framework or a product. It was a quiet way of acknowledging that true intelligence requires both: machines that see patterns, and humans who interpret meaning. They used it sparingly, almost playfully — never as branding, always as perspective.

Because what they were ultimately trying to build wasn't technology.

It was **understanding** — the kind of understanding that was shaped and expressed in **the Myplan8® way**.

The Boardroom That Tested Their Belief

The first true test of their philosophy didn't happen in a lab or technical review. It happened in a bank — one of the largest in the country. The government had given it a bold mandate: *do something meaningful, something green, something future-facing.* The founders walked in with nothing more than a simple deck and an honest intent: show the invisible, make it understandable, and let intelligence guide behaviour gently.

The room was filled with leaders who had shaped India's financial architecture for decades. Fifteen minutes into the discussion, a senior executive leaned forward, genuinely puzzled.

"You mean to say a transaction can reveal environmental behaviour?"

Ms. Imperfect responded with calm conviction. "Ma'am, your transactions already reveal your creditworthiness. They reveal your reliability and trust. If money can reflect financial behaviour, it can also reflect environmental behaviour — because both arise from the same choices."

Mr. Imperfect added, "Money leaves a trail. Each purchase, each bill, each journey — every one of them leaves an environmental shadow. We're simply making that shadow visible."

The silence that followed wasn't resistance — it was the quiet reordering of old thinking.

Many more meetings came after: risk teams, compliance groups, sustainability committees, digital banking leads. Everyone understood their own fragment of the system — but the founders were asking them to see the whole. It took time, explanations, re-explanations, and patient storytelling.

Finally, a senior banker leaned back and said, "Now I see it. This is not carbon calculation. This is behaviour visibility. Financial truth meeting environmental truth."

That sentence opened the door — and climate intelligence stepped in.

The Myplan8® Way — A Philosophy Of Seeing

In a world overflowing with frameworks — life cycle assessments, DEFRA factors, GHG protocols, ESG scoring, SDG mappings, supply-chain audits — people still struggled to understand *impact*. The frameworks existed, yet the comprehension was missing. What the founders began shaping was not a dashboard or a checklist — it was a way of decoding life.

The Myplan8® way was simple, human, and quietly radical. It said:

Humans change when they can finally see themselves.

Visibility precedes responsibility.

Clarity precedes action.

Direction precedes perfection.

The founders saw the world as a tangled map — full of choices, behaviour loops, money trails, misaligned incentives, and unseen emissions. Their philosophy was to untangle it with intelligence that felt more like a companion than a machine.

Woven gently into this worldview were three conceptual pillars — not as product features, but as metaphors for understanding:

A scoring lens to interpret behaviour without judgement.

A navigation logic — a kind of behavioural GPS that recalibrates without shame.

A guidance engine — intelligence that helps people, banks, and businesses understand where they stand and what a better direction looks like.

This interpretive lens — the quiet, poetic backbone beneath climate intelligence — is what they softly called it the **Carbon Intelligence**.

Not a score. Not a feature. Not software.

A way of reading the invisible handwriting beneath everyday life.

The World Was Already Leaning In This Direction

As the founders travelled for climate forums and financial dialogues across continents, they began noticing that the world was drifting toward the same truth — even without naming it.

In **Australia**, sustainability-linked home loans rewarded greener construction with lower interest rates.

In **Germany**, paperless mortgage workflows and energy-efficient data centres reduced operational footprints.

In **Canada**, climate-conscious card rewards nudged people toward sustainable brands.

In **South Korea**, intelligent commuting models influenced green lending decisions.

In **Brazil**, digital wallets enabled everyday users to support Amazon conservation through micro-actions embedded in transactions.

And in India, long before climate intelligence existed, ATMs had taught an entire nation the power of a gentle nudge:

"Skip the slip. Save a tree."

A behavioural revolution written in seven words.

"These aren't isolated experiments," Ms. Imperfect said.

"They're clues."

"And together," Mr. Imperfect added, "they map the direction the world was always meant to take."

Climate Intelligence As A Map, A Compass, A Navigator

Explaining intelligence to people conditioned to think in strict compliance lines was never easy. Systems see rules; intelligence sees relationships. So, the founders embraced metaphors everyone understood.

"Think of climate intelligence like a GPS," Mr. Imperfect would say. "You choose the destination. You choose the journey. But the intelligence shows you the route — the cleaner, safer, more efficient route."

"And if you take a wrong turn," Ms. Imperfect added with a smile, "the system doesn't punish you. It simply recalculates."

This metaphor shifted conversations.

Sustainability no longer felt like a sermon.

It felt like navigation.

Climate intelligence didn't replace free will. It illuminated choice.

It didn't demand perfection. It enabled progress.

It didn't add pressure. It added understanding.

When Banks Discovered Dual ROI

The real transformation began when banks realised climate intelligence wasn't a cost — it was a multiplier.

"For the first time," Ms. Imperfect said during a leadership session, "your financial ROI and your environmental ROI can move together."

Mr. Imperfect explained, "When customers behave greener, risk drops. When businesses improve operational patterns, lending stabilises. When branches digitise, both cost and emissions fall. When visibility increases, decision-making improves."

A banker whispered, "So climate action strengthens profit?"

"That is the beauty of intelligence," she replied.

"And the Myplan8® way," he added, "is letting money and meaning move in the same direction."

That moment — the merging of return on investment with return on impact — made climate intelligence inevitable.

The Human Struggle Behind The System

Despite breakthroughs, the hardest journey wasn't technological — it was human. Regulators worried about oversight. Banks feared disruption. Businesses feared exposure. Customers feared guilt. Investors feared timelines. Engineers feared integration.

But every hesitation refined the philosophy.

Every objection sharpened the lens.

Every debate made Carbon Intelligence gentler, clearer, more human.

"This wasn't built in code," Ms. Imperfect once said. "This was built in conversations."

"And in patience," Mr. Imperfect added.

"And in imperfection," she said.

"And in resilience," he completed.

Climate intelligence wasn't born from certainty.

It was born from empathy.

Becoming Climate-Smart

One late evening, after back-to-back discussions, the founders stood by a window watching the city shimmer — headlights, deliveries, devices charging, offices winding down. A million tiny behaviours forming the atmospheric story above.

"People don't wake up wanting to be sustainable," Ms. Imperfect said softly. "They wake up wanting clarity."

"And once they understand themselves," Mr. Imperfect replied, "they naturally choose better."

That was climate-smart — not perfection, not guilt, not sacrifice, but visibility.

A world where people could finally *see* their patterns.

A world where banks could finally *understand* the behaviour hidden beneath transactions.

A world where businesses could improve without fear or confusion.

A world where intelligence didn't command — it guided.

Didn't overwhelm — it clarified.

Didn't demand perfection — it nurtured progress.

As they gazed at the city's imperfect glow, they felt a shift.

Climate intelligence had begun as a spark between two people.

But now it was becoming something much larger — a way for systems, institutions, and societies to evolve from confusion to clarity, from randomness to direction, from isolated actions to collective momentum.

The next chapter wouldn't be about the two of them.

It would be about **many** — banks, regulators, businesses, and millions of imperfect individuals finally able to navigate a warming world with confidence instead of overwhelm.

The intelligence they built wasn't a destination.

It was a direction.

A compass quietly pointing north.

Chapter 13:

From One To Many

The founders often spoke about Steve Jobs' idea that life only makes sense when the dots connect in hindsight. But unlike most people who admired that philosophy, they had felt compelled to test it — perhaps because both had lived lives where intuition, curiosity, and unlikely intersections had always shaped their decisions. They believed dots were not just memories waiting to be understood; they were choices waiting to be connected.

And now, through the intelligence layer they had built, they were watching those dots connect in real time. Not as a grand revelation, but as a quiet unfolding. The world wasn't changing through grand gestures. It was changing through small recognitions — one dot at a time.

A person sees their Green People Score rise after a single mindful change.

A team celebrates a shared improvement.

A business uncovers an inefficiency once hidden.

A bank notices how maturity aligns with lower risk.

A regulator realises the financial stability of climate visibility.

Dots. Becoming lines.

Lines. Becoming pathways.

Pathways. Becoming a new system.

This was not evolution by force.

This was evolution by understanding.

The First Dot: Individual Awareness

Behavioural science tells us that humans rarely shift because of rules; they shift because something suddenly becomes visible.

When people saw their Green People Scores for the first time, they did not see guilt — they saw themselves.

A person realised that their impulse shopping spiked their environmental behaviour score more than expected. Not a lecture. Not a warning. Just a reflection.

Another noticed that reducing two weekly cab rides altered their pattern.

Someone else found joy in discovering that mindful eating habits genuinely influenced their personal score.

This is the same mechanism behind so many cultural changes in history:

1. When calorie counts first appeared on menus, people began making different choices not because they were told to — but because the number changed the mental model.

2. When cars started including fuel-efficiency meters, drivers naturally began conserving fuel.
3. When step counters became commonplace on phones, millions unknowingly shifted their walking habits.

Humans change when the invisible becomes visible.

The Green People Score did not demand change — it allowed it.

And once one person sees the shift, the people around them sense it too.

The Second Dot: Communities Learn To Move Together

Communities do not need rules to adapt; they need rhythm.

Groups began discussing their collective behaviour with a surprising sense of camaraderie.

Neighbours gently encouraged each other.

School children compared their small improvements with delight.

Youth-led groups began championing imperfect environmental habits simply because the narrative felt attainable.

It wasn't activism.

It wasn't perfection.

It was community consciousness — the kind that arises when a shared mirror is placed before many.

The founders would often reflect on it:

"Behaviour spreads like warmth," Ms. Imperfect said one day.

"And warmth doesn't need instruction," Mr. Imperfect added. "It travels because it feels right."

This was not a movement yet.

But it was becoming one.

The Third Dot: Workplaces Find Their Identity

If homes shape habit, workplaces shape identity.

So, when companies began engaging with both the Green People Score and the Green Business Score, behaviour scaling grew sharper, faster, and more intentional.

Employees began noticing their own patterns reflected at work.

Companies found purpose in rewarding climate-positive habits.

Green Loyalty Programs emerged — not as promotions, but as reinforcement systems.

Rewards shifted from traditional shopping coupons to climate-positive vouchers redeemable with sustainable brands, green merchants, or low-impact services.

These incentives were not bribes.

They were behavioural cues — the same kind that built gym cultures, reading cultures, even digital-wellness habits.

A department head told the founders,

"People feel proud when their choices matter. That's the shift."

Workplaces began to internalise an idea that had been waiting for its time:

culture changes when incentives reflect values.

And once workplaces changed, businesses found themselves pulled into the next transformation.

The Fourth Dot: Businesses See The System

Behind every business lies a labyrinth — suppliers, materials, logistics, policies, energy, waste.

For decades these layers had been invisible.

The Green Business Score finally illuminated them.

Suddenly, organisations could see which choices aligned with global climate directions and which ones put them at long-term risk.

This visibility aligned almost perfectly with the global policy wave of 2022–2025.

Corporate Sustainability Reporting Directive (CSRD)

This major global shift required thousands of companies to measure and disclose environmental impact with a new level of accuracy.

For the first time, businesses were legally obligated to present climate data the same way they present financial data.

It turned sustainability from storytelling into accounting.

Carbon Border Adjustment Mechanism (CBAM)

A new rule that essentially said:

If your product is polluting, the cost will follow it across borders.

It reshaped export strategies, forcing companies to examine their supply chains — not because of climate ethics, but because trade survival required it.

International Sustainability Standards Board (ISSB)

These standards harmonised global reporting.

Businesses were now expected to speak one language about risk, emissions, scenario analysis, and climate impact.

Science-Based Targets initiatives (SBTi)

Companies and financial institutions had to align targets with science — not with marketing claims.

It became a reset button for credibility.

Auditable national frameworks

Many countries implemented audited sustainability disclosures (similar to BRSR Core).

Climate data now had to be verifiable, accurate, and traceable.

Principles for Responsible Banking (UNEP FI)

Financial institutions were expected to align portfolios with planetary limits.

Suddenly, businesses needed maturity — not to impress customers, but to maintain banking relationships.

The founders realised something profound:

Policies were not driving behaviour alone.

Visibility was enabling policy.

Businesses could see themselves clearly for the first time.

And once they saw, they moved.

The Fifth Dot: Banks — The Great Multiplier

Banks sit at the nexus of the world.

Every person touches them.

Every business depends on them.

Every policymaker relies on them.

Banks were the ultimate "one to many."

When climate intelligence reached banking institutions, the shift was immediate and exponential:

1. Lending models began factoring climate maturity.
2. Capital started flowing toward low-risk, low-emission businesses.
3. Customers received nudges toward better choices.
4. Digital journeys replaced carbon-heavy physical processes.

5. Banks realised lower emissions often meant lower risk — and lower risk meant better financial outcomes.

A leader from a financial institution told the founders:

"You've shown us that climate visibility is business visibility."

This was the birth of a new logic:

Dual ROI — Return on Investment + Return on Impact.

Profit and planet no longer conflicted.

They aligned.

Banks multiplied every behavioural shift.

One insight became many decisions.

One score became many corrections.

One change became many consequences.

And once banks moved, regulators could not ignore the momentum.

The Sixth Dot: Regulators Become Architects

Regulators stepped in not out of obligation, but out of clarity.

They realised climate intelligence wasn't environmental protection.

It was economic protection.

Regulators began requiring:

1. Climate stress tests,

2. Maturity-based risk scoring,
3. Transparent climate disclosures,
4. Auditable environmental metrics,
5. Alignment with global sustainability frameworks,
6. Capital buffers tied to climate risk.

Climate policy was no longer environmental.

It was infrastructural.

A policymaker told the founders,

"This is not about saving the planet. This is about saving the financial system that lives on it."

The founders carried that line with quiet pride.

Incentives — The Engine Of Many

Visibility is the mirror.

Intelligence is the compass.

But incentives are the engine.

The founders expanded the incentivisation layer of the Myplan8® way deliberately, carefully, and with behavioural science at its core.

They built systems where:

1. Climate-positive actions earned verifiable climate credits,

2. These credits could be redeemed within a green ecosystem,
3. Organisations could run Green Loyalty Programs to reward their workforce,
4. Communities could earn collective benefits based on shared improvements,
5. Businesses saw improved financial terms for higher Green Business Scores,
6. Tokens reflected real-world offsets or removal,
7. Green vouchers became a cultural marker, not a marketing perk.

This was where intelligence evolved into ecosystem.

Where ecosystem evolved into stack.

What began as one idea — visibility — now had guiding layers, scoring layers, incentive layers, and behavioural layers all speaking to one another seamlessly.

Not a product.

A living, breathing architecture.

The Network Forms — And Becomes A Movement

The founders found themselves witnessing something they had never expected:

a world that could finally see itself.

Individuals understood their choices.

Communities found rhythm.

Workplaces formed identity.

Businesses discovered maturity.

Banks multiplied impact.

Regulators shaped coherence.

One to many.

Many to movement.

Movement to momentum.

One evening, looking at the quiet glow of a thousand lives unfolding, Ms. Imperfect whispered,

"This is how it begins – small truths traveling across big systems."

"And once the world can see," Mr. Imperfect replied,

"it finally knows where to go."

They realised that this wasn't about scaling technology.

It was about scaling humanity's ability to understand itself.

Chapter 14:

The Global Transition Moment

The founders often said that if someone wanted to predict the future, they should pay attention to finance, not forecasts. Forecasts tell you what could happen. Finance tells you what *must* happen. And when finance changes, the world has no choice but to follow.

For years, the founders walked into rooms where the world politely tolerated their ideas. The questions were predictable, almost scripted: *Is this really needed? Will people change? Will banks ever care? Is this too idealistic? Is climate action something customers even think about?* These were the old questions — questions shaped by a world that still believed climate action was optional.

But then something flipped.

Almost overnight, the conversations changed tone. The hesitation gave way to urgency. The disbelief gave way to a strange, eager practicality — as if everyone had suddenly realised the old model was collapsing under its own weight. As if global finance had collectively understood that climate transition was no longer a matter of morality, reputation, or goodwill — but survival.

One day, after yet another global briefing landed in their inbox, Ms. Imperfect remarked, "We used to walk into rooms defending the 'why'. Now everyone wants the 'how'."

And Mr. Imperfect added, "Few years ago, they wondered what we were building. Today, they're asking when they can embed it."

Something monumental had shifted.

The world wasn't becoming visionary.

It was becoming vulnerable.

And vulnerability has a way of revealing truth faster than idealism ever could.

The Financial World Begins To Speak A New Language

Across continents, climate policies, financial disclosures, risk frameworks, investor expectations, and sustainability regulations were all beginning to converge toward one undeniable reality:

The financial system is now the engine of global climate transition.

Not the passenger.

Not the partner.

The engine.

Major financial institutions were suddenly required to create credible transition plans — not in loose statements, but in quantified, time-bound, measurable pathways. Banks had to show how their portfolios aligned with net-zero trajectories. Investors demanded insight into transition risk. Regulators insisted on climate scenario analysis. Corporate borrowers were being categorised by climate maturity. And global capital was quietly reorganising itself around climate stability.

A startling statistic stood out everywhere the founders looked: **Financed emissions represented 60–90% of a bank's total emissions footprint.**[1.]

This meant a bank's biggest climate risk wasn't its operations.

It was its clients.

Another number was equally shocking: **More than half of global financial institutions cited inconsistent climate data as their biggest barrier to transition planning.**

Banks were being asked to act — but without the visibility they needed.

This was the exact gap the founders had been solving all along.

They didn't need to build a new philosophy.

The world had adopted theirs on its own.

The Validation Moment

One night, the founders sat on opposite ends of their office couch, scrolling through the latest global policy updates. They looked up at each other almost at the same moment.

"Is it just me," Ms. Imperfect asked, "or is the entire world finally saying exactly what we've built?"

Mr. Imperfect turned his screen toward her. "Look at this," he said. "They're asking banks to track client maturity, guide their trajectory, and prevent climate penalties through better financial visibility. That's everything our intelligence layer already does."

They didn't need applause or external validation.

But seeing the world articulate their philosophy — almost word for word — hit differently.

For the first time, it felt like timing had aligned with truth.

The World Begins To Move As One

In all corners of the financial system, changes were underway.

Large corporates were preparing detailed transition disclosures.

Institutional investors were shifting portfolios toward climate-aligned companies.

Export-driven businesses were adapting internally to avoid border carbon costs.

Insurance companies were evaluating climate risk with unprecedented scrutiny.

Banks were redesigning risk models to capture environmental maturity.

Regulators were connecting financial stability with environmental stability.

Asset managers were integrating climate factors into valuations by default.

Global policy didn't need to be perfect.

It only needed to be directional.

And the direction was clear.

Where there was climate maturity, there would soon be financial preference.

Where there was clarity, there would be capital.

Where there was risk, there would be repricing.

Where there was visibility, there would be transition.

The founders watched the shift with quiet awe.

"This isn't hope anymore," Ms. Imperfect said.

"This is alignment."

"To be honest," Mr. Imperfect replied,

"It feels like the world finally understands the language we've always spoken."

The Missing Bridge The World Didn't Know It Needed

The global transition frameworks were robust, detailed, and ambitious. But they shared the same flaw — they described **what** the world needed to do without explaining **how** institutions could execute it.

Banks needed to classify clients, analyse portfolios, project emissions, map trajectories, avoid penalties, prepare disclosures, and redesign financial products. But doing this manually was expensive, slow, and deeply inconsistent.

"What the world is asking for," Ms. Imperfect said one afternoon, drawing circles on a notepad, "requires a central intelligence spine."

"And a behavioural translation layer," added Mr. Imperfect. "Something that simplifies complex climate signals and gives banks real-time visibility."

"And helps them save money," she added. "That's the part nobody says out loud, but it's the truth."

Because climate transition wasn't only about protecting the planet.

It was about protecting portfolios.

Every global transition guide hinted at this silently:

If businesses failed to mature, banks would pay the price through penalties, losses, provisioning, regulatory shocks, and mispriced capital.

Climate intelligence wasn't only about reducing emissions.

It was about reducing financial exposure.

Every percentage improvement in climate maturity meant:

- fewer penalties for misreporting,
- stronger resilience against shifting policies,
- fewer surprises from new tariffs,
- lower risk-weighted assets,
- lower portfolio volatility,
- reduced compliance cost,
- and eventually, lower cost of capital.

Money was pulling money — but now money was also protecting money.

And for the first time, climate action had a financial return.

The Behavioural Side Of The Global Transition

Systems don't shift because regulations exist.

They shift because behaviour adapts to what becomes visible and valuable.

This was the behavioural secret woven into the global transition:

When businesses saw financial benefits in improving their maturity, they acted faster.

When banks saw their portfolios becoming safer, they doubled down.

When regulators saw alignment, they eased friction rather than increased pressure.

When individuals saw their scores rising, they became more conscious consumers.

Behaviour scaled because it now had meaning — not moral meaning, but measurable meaning.

One senior banker told the founders,

"You didn't give us a climate tool. You gave us a behavioural system."

And he was right.

Climate intelligence wasn't software.

It was perspective.

The World Prepares For A New Financial Backbone

For decades, banks-built systems to understand credit risk, operational risk, and market risk.

Now they needed infrastructure to understand *climate risk* — and do it with the same precision and speed.

But building this infrastructure internally would take years, countless resources, and expertise few institutions possessed.

"What the world needs," said Ms. Imperfect during a late evening walk, "is the climate equivalent of a global financial utility."

"And a way for every bank to plug into it without rebuilding the wheel," Mr. Imperfect added.

"It's not a new bank," she said.

"It's the backbone behind every bank."

"And ultimately," he concluded,

"behind every business, every community, and every person."

This wasn't a product pitch.

It was a global realisation.

The intelligence layer they had built years earlier — once dismissed, once questioned — was now exactly what the world was asking for.

Not a platform.

Not an app.

Not a dashboard.

But an **operating logic**.

A way for the world to think, see, and act coherently.

A way to make financial stability and climate stability indistinguishable.

A way to bring behaviour, policy, risk, and economics into the same room.

The Global Moment Before The Wildfire

As the founders sat together, watching the evening blur into a quiet hum of lights and movement, they sensed something rising — something larger than systems, larger than banks, larger than data or dashboards. It was the feeling of a world finally learning to coordinate with itself.

Not perfectly.

Not uniformly.

But unmistakably.

And that is all meaningful transitions have ever needed.

A few imperfect steps in the same direction.

A few aligned incentives.

A few shared truths.

A few brave institutions willing to see differently.

A few human choices made with a little more clarity.

When these combine, they shift the axis of the world.

Ms. Imperfect exhaled softly, almost in disbelief.

"It feels like the beginning," she said.

Mr. Imperfect nodded.

"Not the beginning of our idea…

the beginning of its impact."

Across industries, across borders, across policies and portfolios, a quiet synchronisation was underway. Climate intelligence was no longer a theory — it was becoming the connective force behind how money moved, how businesses transformed, and how people behaved.

A new kind of momentum had entered the world.

Not loud, not dramatic — but certain.

The certainty that comes when understanding replaces confusion, and when clarity begins to compound like interest.

This was the transition moment:

the point where individual revelations became collective direction,

where direction became alignment,

and alignment began shaping a future that felt not just possible,

but inevitable.

And as the night deepened, they understood something simple and profound:

The world had finally started moving —

and this time, it would not be moving alone.

1. *Source: UNEP FI, 2022; McKinsey Sustainability, 2021.*

Part V
The Movement

Chapter 15:

Imperfect Environmental Impact

When we began this book, we began in the age of steam—an era defined by the industrial heartbeat of progress. Iron rails split landscapes, furnaces lit horizons, and the world grew louder, faster, heavier. The pace of invention was unmatched; the cost of that momentum was invisible. We did not see the darkening skies, the thinning ice, the narrowing margins of safety—not because we didn't care, but because we had never been taught to look.

Environmentalism was, for decades, framed as a pursuit of perfection: zero waste, zero plastic, zero emissions, zero excuses. But perfection is a language most people never learn. And somewhere between the pressure to be flawless and the guilt of being human, the world lost its way.

The revolution that now rises is built on a gentler truth.

Imperfect environmentalism—powered by everyday transactions—has the force to reshape the planet more profoundly than any perfect ideology ever could.

Because nothing is more universal than imperfection,

and nothing is more constant than the way money moves through our lives.

Every swipe, tap, bill, transfer, subscription, or salary is a clue—a behavioural fingerprint. When these clues become visible, they form a map. When interpreted through intelligence, they become a compass. And when acted upon collectively, they become a movement.

This was the question the founders carried long before it became evident to the world:

What if every transaction could become a climate action?

The World That Finally Woke Up

For years, that question lived ahead of its time. But slowly, global patterns shifted in ways that echoed the founders' thinking.

Banks discovered that **60–90% of their climate exposure comes from financed emissions.** [1] Corporations realised that **up to 80% of their impact hides in their supply chains.**[2] Regulators acknowledged that inconsistent climate data is now the largest barrier to global transition efforts.[3]

These numbers revealed the same truth:

the world wasn't failing due to apathy,

it was failing due to invisibility.

When the founders saw global institutions articulating the very gaps their system was designed to solve, it didn't feel like vindication—it felt like alignment.

"Every line leads to the same missing piece," Ms. Imperfect said, scanning a global report.

"And we have already built it."

Mr. Imperfect nodded. "The world is finally learning the language we wrote years ago."

A Small Example That Shows A Global Possibility

To understand imperfect environmentalism, imagine one small action.

Let's take **an indicative example**.

Suppose one person reduces just **two high-emission deliveries a week** by choosing a lower-impact option instead. A typical high-emission last-mile delivery emits around **1–1.5 kg CO_2e**. Two avoided deliveries per week equal roughly **150 kg CO_2e saved annually**.

Now imagine just **1% of global adults**—around 60 million people—making the same small choice.

The indicative impact would be around **9 million metric tons of CO_2e** avoided every year, equivalent to removing **approximately 2 million cars** from the road.[4]

One small action.

By a tiny fraction of humanity.

Expanding into an impact that resembles planetary-scale mathematics.

Now compound that with food habits, commute changes, electricity behaviour, procurement shifts, banking incentives, and regulatory guidance. Small actions stop being symbolic and start becoming structural.

This is the arithmetic of imperfect environmentalism.

The Three Circles Of The Future

If you were to draw the world we're now entering, it would look like three circles intersecting: **People. Payments. Planet.**

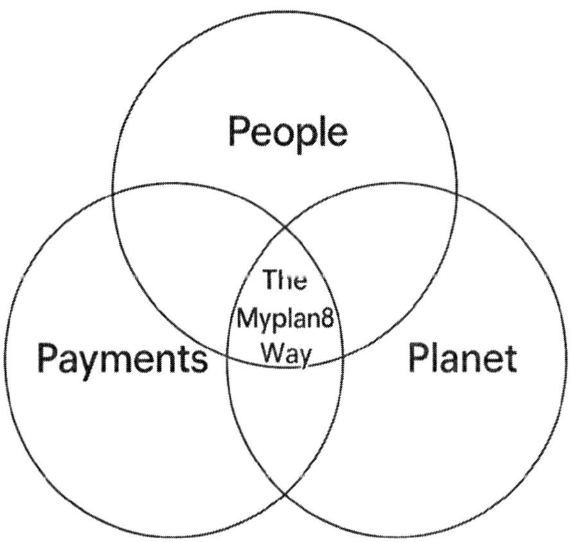

People shape choices.

Payments reflect choices.

Planet absorbs choices.

And at the centre where all three circles meet sits **The Myplan8® Way**: a philosophy built not on flawless conduct but on measurable clarity, navigable intelligence, and empowered imperfection.

The **Green People Score** gives individuals visibility into their lifestyle.

The **Green Business Score** provides companies with truth, maturity, and direction.

The **Climate Intelligence Layer** guides banks toward smarter, safer portfolios.

And regulators receive data they can trust—coherent, consistent, credible.

The ecosystem stops functioning as fragmented actors

and begins functioning as a single, synchronized organism.

The Human Engine Behind Systemic Change

People are not unwilling—only uninformed. That has always been the founders' belief. Humans behave better when they can see.

A map changes the way you walk through a city.

A compass changes how you navigate the mountains.

A score changes how you evaluate yourself.

When individuals saw their impact, they adjusted.

When businesses saw their maturity, they improved.

When banks saw their exposure, they recalibrated.

When regulators saw clarity, they strengthened the system.

Climate action shifted from an overwhelming moral burden to a practical daily rhythm.

Not perfect, but possible.

Not absolute, but achievable.

Not heroic, but human.

The Call That Belongs To Every Reader

If you are reading these lines, you are part of what comes next.

If you are reading these lines, the revolution is no longer abstract.

It is now *personal.*

And the question is no longer, *"What can someone do?"*

It is, *"What can I do right now?"*

That is why the founders built **Myplan8®**, not as an app or a dashboard, but as an entry point into this new way of living.

A doorway into imperfect environmentalism.

If you are an individual:

You can download the **Myplan8® app** and begin immediately:

- See your **Green People Score**—a real-time mirror of your lifestyle emissions
- Understand the impact of your spending: groceries, food delivery, flights, fashion, mobility
- Receive **AI-powered guidance** for small, realistic shifts
- Track your weekly and monthly improvement without guilt
- Earn **Green Rewards** for positive actions
- Join community challenges and compare your impact with friends, families, and workplaces

Climate action becomes not a burden, but a rhythm—woven into every transaction you already make.

If you are a business, maturity is your greatest asset. Transparency is trust, built it with:

- A **Green Business Score**, reflecting operational maturity, governance, lifestyle impact of employees, and product-level footprint
- A unified **climate-intelligence dashboard** for procurement, supply chain, and ESG tracking
- Ability to integrate **green incentives** for employees
- A pathway to become a **Green Place to Work**
- Instant visibility into hotspots, reduction pathways, and projected savings

- A tool to demonstrate commitment to investors, lenders, and regulators

You don't guess your impact; you see it.

You don't chase compliance; you navigate it.

If you are a bank or financial institution, your decisions will shape the next century:

Banks can:

- Integrate the **Climate Intelligence Layer** behind their core systems
- Offer customers transaction-level climate insights
- Score SMEs and corporate clients through **Green Business Scores** for lending
- Reduce exposure to climate-related financial risks
- Deliver green financing products confidently
- Align automatically with global frameworks like ESG, SDG, NGFS, EU taxonomy, and more

Your institution becomes not just a lender,

but a **navigator of the low-carbon transition**.

If you are a regulator or policymaker, you hold the pen that writes the rules. Empower the frameworks that work with:

- A unified language for reporting
- A consistent mechanism to evaluate banks and businesses

- A pathway to replace fragmented disclosures with a cohesive ecosystem
- Real-time climate intelligence that reflects actual behaviour, not static PDFs

Regulation becomes not reactive, but **future-ready**.

And if you are simply a human being living on this fragile, beautiful planet—

know that revolutions are built by imperfect people who refuse to wait for perfect conditions.

The Circle Completes

When we started this journey, the world was defined by the roar of machines and the quiet melting of ice—a contrast so stark it had become invisible. Today, nothing has changed in the physical world. The trains still run. The factories still hum. The world is still imperfect.

But *we* have changed.

Now we know how to see.

What was once invisible is now illuminated.

What was once overwhelming is now navigable.

What was once impossible is now inevitable.

The circle completes itself:

from unchecked consumption

to conscious transaction.

From invisible impact

to visible intelligence.

From isolated effort

to collective movement.

And at the centre of that circle is the most powerful idea of this book:

The planet will not be saved by perfect people,

but by imperfect people who choose differently—

one transaction, one habit, one heartbeat at a time.

Epilogue -The Quiet Shift

Most revolutions announce themselves loudly.

This one won't.

It will happen quietly—

in the moment someone checks their score for the first time,

in a business choosing a greener supplier,

in a bank shifting capital toward maturity,

in a regulator recognizing coherence,

in a family changing one small habit,

in communities celebrating better choices,

in children growing up knowing that climate action

is not an occasional gesture but an everyday rhythm.

The true revolution will not be the scoring system,

or the intelligence layer,

or the frameworks,

or even the inventions.

The true revolution will be the world learning a new pattern—

where money no longer moves without meaning,

where behaviour no longer hides from consequence,

and where climate action is not an effort

but the natural pulse of life.

One day, someone will look back and ask,

"When did it begin?"

And the answer will be simple:

It began when the world finally saw itself.

It began when imperfection became participation.

It began when you turned the final page of this book

carrying a new understanding—

and decided that your next action would matter.

Because it does.

Because it always has.

And because now,

finally,

it can.

1. *Source: UNEP FI, 2022; McKinsey Sustainability, 2021.*
2. *Source: CDP Global Supply Chain Report, 202.*
3. *Source: NGFS, 2023.*
4. *Emission equivalency based on EPA guidelines, 2023.*

Where to Find the Myplan8® Way

To begin your own journey:

☞ **Individuals:**

Download the **Myplan8® App**

(iOS & Android — search *Myplan8*, or visit www.myplan8.com or www.myplan8.earth)

☞ **Businesses, Bank & Financial Institution or Regulators, Policy Think Tanks, and Research Bodies:**

Connect with the team behind it at info@myplan8.earth or visit www.myplan8.com or www.myplan8.earth

No step is too small.

Every action counts.

And now, every action is finally visible.

Appendix

This appendix compiles key frameworks, scientific concepts, and structural elements referenced across the book. It serves as a supporting reference for readers who want deeper clarity on the systems that shape environmental intelligence, green scoring, and climate-led financial innovation.

A. Global Environmental Frameworks Referenced in the Book

1. UNFCCC — United Nations Framework Convention on Climate Change

A global treaty that forms the foundation of international climate negotiations, including Paris Agreement commitments, Nationally Determined Contributions (NDCs), and global stocktake mechanisms.

2. Paris Agreement (2015)

A legally binding international treaty adopted by 196 countries, committing to limit global warming to 1.5 2°C.

The Agreement also mandates transparent reporting, long-term strategies, and sector-wide climate transition plans.

3. GHG Protocol — Greenhouse Gas Protocol

The world's most widely used carbon accounting framework, dividing emissions into:

- **Scope 1** – Direct emissions
- **Scope 2** – Indirect energy-related emissions
- **Scope 3** – All other value-chain emissions

4. DEFRA Emission Factors

Annual datasets published by the UK government that quantify emissions associated with different fuels, activities, and materials.

5. SDGs — Sustainable Development Goals

17 global goals established by the United Nations, ranging from climate action (SDG 13) to responsible consumption (SDG 12), equality, clean energy, and economic resilience.

6. ESG — Environmental, Social, Governance Reporting

Corporate disclosures used by investors, regulators, and markets to assess sustainability risks, performance, and governance quality.

7. Digital Product Passport (EU DPP)

An emerging regulatory cornerstone requiring companies to disclose the lifecycle footprint of products, from raw materials to disposal.

8. CBAM — Carbon Border Adjustment Mechanism

A European Union policy imposing fees on imported goods based on their embedded carbon footprint, influencing global supply chains.

9. SBTi — Science-Based Targets Initiative

A global effort helping companies align climate strategies with planetary boundaries.

B. Technical Foundations of the Green Scoring System

1. Lifecycle Assessment (LCA)

A science-based method that evaluates environmental impact from raw material extraction → manufacturing → distribution → use → disposal.

2. Climate Intelligence Layer

The AI + behavioural + financial integration system described in the book — the "navigation engine" that helps banks, businesses, and individuals interpret impact.

3. Environmental Quotient (EQ)

The combined framework of Green People Score + Green Business Score — forming a unified behavioural and structural measure of climate maturity.

4. Green People Score

An individual's environmental behaviour score based on daily transactions, lifestyle patterns, and spending habits.

5. Green Business Score

A structural maturity score for businesses based on lifecycle, governance, ESG alignment, climate risk, supply chain, and operations.

6. Imperfect Environmentalism Model

A behavioural philosophy that prioritizes small, consistent actions over perfectionism, turning every transaction into a micro-action for climate good.

C. Banking, Finance & Policy References

1. Financed Emissions

The emissions banks are indirectly responsible for through lending, investments, and capital allocation.

2. Climate-Related Financial Disclosure Norms

Emerging regulations across Europe, India, and the US that require climate risk transparency.

3. Digital Banking Journeys

Modern financial pathways (UPI, NFC, cardless withdrawals, digital onboarding) that significantly reduce physical operational emissions.

4. Green Financing

Lending or investment directed towards environmentally positive projects, often guided by sustainability-linked loan frameworks.

D. Mandatory & Voluntary Reporting Frameworks in Global Sustainability

1. CSRD — Corporate Sustainability Reporting Directive (EU)

A landmark EU directive requiring more than 50,000 companies to disclose detailed sustainability data, including:

- climate risks
- emissions
- transition plans
- environmental and social impacts
- governance oversight
- double materiality assessment (impact + financial risk)

CSRD is enforced through the ESRS (European Sustainability Reporting Standards).

2. ESRS — European Sustainability Reporting Standards

These standards define *how* companies must report under CSRD:

- ESRS E1 — Climate Change
- ESRS E2 — Pollution
- ESRS E3 — Water & Marine Resources
- ESRS E4 — Biodiversity
- ESRS E5 — Circular Economy
- ESRS S1–S4 — Social Standards

- ESRS G1 — Governance

They require companies to disclose:

- Scope 1, 2, 3 emissions
- Transition plans
- Forward-looking scenario analysis
- Climate financial risk
- Environmental dependencies

3. CBAM — Carbon Border Adjustment Mechanism (EU)

A tax on imported goods based on their embedded carbon footprint.

Targets high-carbon sectors such as:

- steel
- cement
- aluminium
- fertilizers
- electricity
- hydrogen

CBAM directly affects global supply chains, forcing companies to calculate and disclose product-level emissions.

4. TCFD — Task Force on Climate-Related Financial Disclosures

TCFD pioneered the global climate-risk reporting movement and focuses on:

- governance
- strategy
- risk management
- targets and metrics

Its principles now underpin multiple regulatory systems worldwide.

5. ISSB — International Sustainability Standards Board (IFRS Foundation)

ISSB introduced two major standards:

- **IFRS S1** — General Sustainability Disclosure Requirements
- **IFRS S2** — Climate-Related Disclosure Requirements

These are rapidly becoming the **global baseline** for climate reporting.

ISSB integrates lessons from:

- TCFD
- SASB
- CDSB
- GRI interoperability

6. EU Taxonomy for Sustainable Activities

A classification system defining which economic activities are environmentally sustainable.

Covers:

- climate change mitigation
- climate change adaptation
- circularity
- water protection
- biodiversity
- pollution prevention

Used heavily in green finance, bonds, and transition planning.

7. NGFS — Network for Greening the Financial System

A global coalition of central banks that provides:

- climate scenario pathways
- stress-testing frameworks
- sector-level emission trajectories

Banks use NGFS data to model climate risk in lending.

8. SBTi — Science-Based Targets Initiative (Corporate + Financial)

Provides scientifically aligned pathways to:

- reduce emissions
- set net-zero targets
- align with Paris Agreement goals

Includes **SBTi for Financial Institutions (FIs)**, enabling banks to manage financed emissions.

9. SEBI BRSR — Business Responsibility and Sustainability Reporting (India)

Mandatory ESG reporting system for the top-listed companies in India.

Covers:

- environment
- employee welfare
- corporate governance
- ethical supply chains
- climate disclosures

Includes **BRSR Core**, a standardized assurance-ready subset.

10. SEC Climate Disclosure Rule (USA)

The U.S. Securities & Exchange Commission now requires:

- climate risk reporting
- Scope 1 & 2 emissions
- governance oversight disclosures
- material climate impacts on operations

11. EU Digital Product Passport (DPP)

A major initiative from the European Commission requiring companies to disclose:

- full product lifecycle emissions
- material sourcing
- repairability

- recyclability
- circularity metrics

This will redefine global manufacturing and supply chains.

12. GRI — Global Reporting Initiative

One of the earliest ESG reporting standards, focusing on:

- material impacts
- sustainability context
- stakeholder inclusiveness

Still widely used across industries globally.

13. CDP — Carbon Disclosure Project

A global platform where companies voluntarily disclose:

- emissions
- climate risks
- water usage
- deforestation risks

Used by investors, banks, and regulators.

14. TNFD — Taskforce on Nature-Related Financial Disclosures

An emerging framework focused on:

- biodiversity
- ecosystem services
- nature-related risks

TNFD complements climate disclosures with ecological integrity.

15. Transition Plans (UK, EU, Global)

Banks and businesses must now create:

- detailed decarbonization pathways
- capital allocation strategies
- governance structures
- interim targets (2030/2035)
- risk mitigation strategies

The UK's Transition Plan Taskforce (TPT) sets one of the most advanced frameworks.

16. Green Bond & Sustainability-Linked Loan Principles

Global financial guidelines by:

- ICMA (International Capital Market Association)
- LMA (Loan Market Association)

Used for raising climate-positive capital.

17. Carbon Accounting Systems Used Worldwide

Including:

- ISO 14067 (Carbon Footprint of Products)
- ISO 14064 (GHG quantification and reporting)
- PCAF (Partnership for Carbon Accounting Financials) — especially for banks

Glossary (Alphabetical)

A

AI — Artificial Intelligence

Computer systems capable of analysing data, recognizing patterns, and generating insights — used in the book to interpret climate impact at scale.

AI² — Artificial + Assisted Intelligence

A Myplan8® term representing a blend of artificial intelligence with human-centred, behavioural interpretation. It is the intelligence powering the Climate Intelligence Layer.

Apple Finance Ecosystem

Referenced as an example of how consumer products evolve into financial ecosystems — proving how design + finance + behaviour influence sustainability.

B

BKC — Bandra-Kurla Complex

Mumbai's premier financial district, referenced as the location of the founders' pivotal meeting with their first angel investor.

BRSR — Business Responsibility and Sustainability Reporting (India)

Mandatory ESG reporting framework enforced by SEBI for large Indian corporations.

BRSR Core

A subset of BRSR disclosures requiring assured, standardised, comparable sustainability metrics.

C

CBAM — Carbon Border Adjustment Mechanism

EU policy imposing carbon-based import taxes to ensure fair competition and global decarbonization.

CDP — Carbon Disclosure Project

A global disclosure system for reporting climate, water, and forest-related impacts.

Circular Economy

A system where resources are reused, repaired, repurposed, or recycled instead of discarded.

Climate Intelligence

The interpretive system (method + AI^2 + behaviour + finance + lifecycle science) that converts raw data into guidance and scoring.

CO_2 — Carbon Dioxide

A greenhouse gas released from burning fossil fuels, deforestation, and many industrial activities.

CO_2e — Carbon Dioxide Equivalent

A standardized measure that converts all greenhouse gases into the warming equivalent of CO_2.

CSRD — Corporate Sustainability Reporting Directive

EU's mandatory sustainability reporting law that applies to over 50,000 companies.

D

DPP — Digital Product Passport

A European regulation requiring complete lifecycle transparency for manufactured goods.

DEFRA — Department for Environment, Food & Rural Affairs (UK)

Publishes global-standard emission factors used for carbon calculations.

E

ESG — Environmental, Social, Governance

A set of performance indicators used by investors, regulators, and markets to assess the sustainability and ethics of companies.

ESRS — European Sustainability Reporting Standards

Standards under CSRD defining how companies must disclose sustainability information.

EU Taxonomy

A classification system determining which economic activities qualify as environmentally sustainable.

Externalities

Hidden costs or benefits of an activity that affect society but are not reflected in financial transactions (e.g., pollution).

F

Financed Emissions

Indirect emissions caused by loans, investments, and financial portfolios — a major concern for banks.

FinTech — Financial Technology

Technology-driven financial services like apps, digital banking, UPI, cardless payments, etc.

G

GHG — Greenhouse Gases

Gases that trap heat in the atmosphere, including CO_2, methane, nitrous oxide, and others.

GHG Protocol

The world's most widely used framework for measuring and reporting emissions.

GPS (Environmental Navigation)

A metaphor used throughout the book to describe real-time direction and guidance in sustainability journeys.

Green Business Score

Myplan8®'s scoring system evaluating a company's environmental maturity across lifecycle, governance, emissions, supply chain, ESG, and climate risk.

Green People Score

Myplan8®'s behaviour-based environmental score for individuals, reflecting lifestyle patterns and transaction-linked impact.

I

IFRS S1 / S2 — International Sustainability Standards Board

Global standards for climate and sustainability disclosure.

Impact Investing

Investing in companies or projects that generate positive environmental or social outcomes.

Imperfect Environmentalism

The philosophy that small, repeated, realistic actions create more impact than unsustainable perfectionism.

L

LCA — Life Cycle Assessment

A scientific method used to analyse environmental impact across a product's entire life cycle.

M

Methane (CH_4)

A potent greenhouse gas emitted from food waste, agriculture, and landfills—far more warming than CO_2.

Myplan8®

The climate-intelligence ecosystem designed by the founders, enabling individuals, businesses, banks, and regulators to turn transactions into climate action.

N

Net Zero

A balance between emissions produced and emissions removed from the atmosphere.

NGFS — Network for Greening the Financial System

A global group of central banks creating climate-risk scenarios for the financial sector.

P

PCAF — Partnership for Carbon Accounting Financials

A widely used framework for banks to measure financed emissions.

Product Footprint

Total environmental impact associated with a product's lifecycle — raw materials to disposal.

R

ROI — Return on Investment

Financial gain relative to cost; used in the book alongside *Return on Impact.*

Return on Impact (Green ROI)

Impact-based value measured through reduced emissions, improved scores, and climate-aligned outcomes.

S

SASB — Sustainability Accounting Standards Board

Provides industry-specific sustainability reporting standards.

Scope 1, 2, 3

GHG Protocol categories defining direct, energy-related, and value-chain emissions.

SDGs — Sustainable Development Goals

17 global goals established by the United Nations for a sustainable future.

SEBI — Securities and Exchange Board of India

Regulator responsible for BRSR and ESG governance in India.

Sustainable Finance

Financial mechanisms supporting environmentally positive activities.

SBTi — Science-Based Targets Initiative

Provides emission-reduction pathways aligned with climate science.

T

TCFD — Task Force on Climate-Related Financial Disclosures

A framework requiring transparent reporting of climate risks and governance.

TNFD — Taskforce on Nature-Related Financial Disclosures

A framework for reporting nature and biodiversity-related risks.

Transition Finance

Capital used to support gradual, credible decarbonization of companies.

Transition Plans

Long-term corporate/banking strategies outlining how they will meet climate targets.

U

UPI — Unified Payments Interface

India's real-time digital payment system enabling fast, cashless transactions; referenced as an example of digital journeys with lower operational carbon footprints.

V

Value Chain Emissions

Emissions generated across the entire chain of suppliers, vendors, logistics, distribution, and end-users.

W

Waste Footprint

The environmental impact created by waste generation, including methane emissions from food waste.

Z

Zero Waste

A sustainability philosophy focused on reuse, recycling, and avoiding landfill.
